THE CURLYTOPS AND THEIR PETS

Or, *Uncle Toby's Strange Collection*

I0616975

HOWARD R. GARIS

1st WORLD
LIBRARY
Literary Society

The Curlytops and Their Pets

Howard R. Garis

© 1st World Library, 2007
PO Box 2211
Fairfield, IA 52556
www.1stworldlibrary.com
First Edition

LCCN: 2007934157

Softcover ISBN: 978-1-4218-9651-9
Hardcover ISBN: 978-1-4218-9751-6
eBook ISBN: 978-1-4218-9551-2

Purchase *"The Curlytops and Their Pets"*
as a traditional bound book at:
www.1stWorldLibrary.com/purchase.asp?ISBN=978-1-4218-9651-9

1st World Library is a literary, educational organization
dedicated to:

- Creating a free internet library of downloadable ebooks

- Hosting writing competitions and offering book publishing
  scholarships.

Interested in more 1st World Library books? contact:
literacy@1stworldlibrary.com
Check us out at: www.1stworldlibrary.com

1st World Library Literary Society

Giving Back to the World

"If you want to work on the core problem, it's early school literacy."

- James Barksdale, former CEO of Netscape

"No skill is more crucial to the future of a child, or to a democratic and prosperous society, than literacy."

- Los Angeles Times

"Literacy... means far more than learning how to read and write... The aim is to transmit... knowledge and promote social participation."

- UNESCO

"Literacy is not a luxury, it is a right and a responsibility. If our world is to meet the challenges of the twenty-first century we must harness the energy and creativity of all our citizens."

- President Bill Clinton

"Parents should be encouraged to read to their children, and teachers should be equipped with all available techniques for teaching literacy, so the varying needs and capacities of individual kids can be taken into account."

- Hugh Mackay

CONTENTS

CHAPTER I

UNCLE TOBY'S LETTER

"What you going to put on your ship, Ted?"

"Oh, swords and guns and gunpowder and soldiers. What you going to load on your ship, Jan?"

"Oranges and lemons and pineapples," answered the little girl, who was playing with her brother at sailing boats in the brook that ran back of the house. "And maybe I'll have gold and diamonds and chocolate cake on my ship, Teddy," went on Janet Martin.

"If you do I'll be a pirate and sink your ship! Oh, Jan, let's play that! I'll be a pirate!"

Teddy Martin jumped up so suddenly from the bank of the brook, where he was loading his ship with what he called "swords, guns and gunpowder," that he tipped the vessel over and the whole cargo was spilled into the water.

"Oh, look what you did!" cried Janet. "Your gunpowder will be all wet!"

"I'm not ready to play the pirate game yet," explained Teddy.

"Anyhow, I can get more powder."

This would be easy enough, it seemed, as the children were only pretending that stones, pebbles and bits of sticks were the cargoes of their toy ships, and, as Teddy had said, he could easily get more stones. The brook was filled with them.

"Where are you going?" Janet called after her brother, as she saw him hurrying toward the house, which was out of sight behind the trees and bushes that grew on the edge of the brook.

"I'm going to get a black flag so I can be a pirate and sink your ship with gold, diamonds and chocolate cakes on!" answered Teddy over his shoulder as he ran on.

"I—I don't guess I want you to be a pirate," said Janet slowly, as she looked at her ship, on which the pebbles, stones and bits of wood were neatly arranged in piles. "I'm not going to play that game! I don't want you to be a pirate, Ted! It's too scary!"

But her brother was beyond the reach of her voice now, hurrying toward the house after his "black pirate flag." Janet shoved her ship out from the shore—her ship laden with diamonds, gold and chocolate cakes. Of course it was not a real ship. The Curlytops would not have had half as much fun with real ships as they were having with the pieces of boards which they were making believe were steamers and sailing vessels.

"I'll sail my ship away down to the end of the brook before Ted gets back to be a pirate," said Janet to herself, as, with a long stick, she directed the flat board which was piled high with brook-pebbles. "Then when he comes back he can't sink it."

Janet pushed her ship slowly at first, and then a little faster, moving it along by means of the stick while she stood on the bank. Then, hearing a noise in the bushes behind her, she thrust harder on the stick.

"I don't want Teddy to pirate my ship!" she thought. "I'll fool him! I'll sail it around the bend, and then I'll hide behind the big buttonball tree and he won't know where I've gone!"

In order to do this Janet wanted to make her ship go as fast as possible, so she shoved harder and harder on the stick. And then, all of a sudden, her ship upset.

With a splash the stones, pebbles and bits of wood went into the brook. The whole cargo was sunk and lost as surely as if Ted's pirate vessel had captured that of his sister. That is, everything sank but the ship itself and the cargo of little sticks, some of which Janet was pretending were chocolate cakes. Even at that, I suppose, the chocolate cakes would be wet and soggy. And soggy chocolate cake isn't good to eat. The best thing you can do with it is to make it into a pudding.

"Oh, Ted! look what you made me do," cried Janet sadly, as she saw the ship, which she had loaded with such care, capsized and cleared of its cargo. "It's all your fault!"

And then she started in surprise as a babyish voice replied:

"I 'idn't do nuffin! I 'ust comed! What's matter, Jan?"

"Oh, it's you, is it, Trouble?" asked the girl, as she turned and saw, instead of Teddy, her smaller brother William, more often called "Trouble," because he was in it so often.

"Yep! Me is here!" announced Trouble. Sometimes he talked more correctly than this, and his mother had told Janet and Teddy to try to cure him of his baby talk and the wrong use of words. But Ted and Jan thought it was "cute" to hear Trouble say queer things, so they did not mend his talk as often as they might.

"I thought you were Ted," went on Janet. "Did you see him? He went up to the house to get a flag."

"Flag," returned Trouble, in a questioning voice. "Goin' to be soldiers an' have a 'rade?" He meant parade, of course.

"No, we aren't going to have a parade now, Trouble," said Janet. "Ted went to get a black flag to be a pirate, so he could sink my ship that was loaded with diamonds, gold and chocolate cakes."

"I want chocolate cake—two pieces!" demanded Trouble, who had ears only for the last words of his sister.

"There wasn't any chocolate cake—really, dear," explained the little girl, as she ruffled up her curly hair. "Ted and I were just pretending. He is going to have a pirate ship. I didn't want him to get mine, so I was shoving it hard down the brook, but I made it go too fast and it upset. Now I've got to load my ship all over again."

"I want s'ip!" demanded William, as Jan began to guide her empty vessel back to shore by means of the long stick. "Trouble have a s'ip?" he asked.

"Yes, you may have a ship, and play with us," Janet said, and as she was looking about for a board which might serve her little brother to play with, she heard someone coming through the bushes.

Howard R. Garis

"I guess this is Ted," thought Janet. "Anyhow he can't sink my ship now. I did it myself."

It was her older brother, and he now came bursting through the shrubbery that lined the bank of the brook, holding in his hands a piece of black cloth.

"I got the pirate flag!" cried Teddy. "Whoop-la! Now I'm going to sink your ship! Why, what happened?" he asked, as he saw that Janet's craft was empty. "Did Trouble upset it?"

"No, I did it myself," Janet answered. "But I didn't mean to. I was trying to hide it from you, 'cause I don't want you to be a pirate and upset my ship full of chocolate cakes."

"Oh, I must be a pirate! Here's the black flag and I must be a pirate!" shouted Teddy. "Whoop! I'm a pirate! I'm a pirate!"

"Hoo! Hoo! Hoop!" yelled Trouble, trying to make as much noise as his brother.

"You sound more like an Indian than you do a pirate," said Janet, as she began to pile more pebbles on the board that was her ship.

"Well, Indians and pirates are 'most the same," declared Teddy. "Wait till you see my ship, with swords and guns and powder! It will blow your ship out of the water, and I'll have a black flag on it and everything! Whoop!"

"I'm not going to play if you upset my ship, now there!" and Janet pouted her lips and ceased loading pebbles aboard her craft.

Teddy, who was cutting a flagstaff with his knife, stopped to look at her. If Janet was going to act this way, and not send out her ship, there was no use in being a pirate. What fun could even a make-believe pirate have if there were no ships to sink?

Teddy thought of this, and then he said:

"All right, Jan, I won't be a pirate if you don't want me to. But I'll have a black flag, anyhow, and maybe I'll be a pirate some other time. Let's have a race with our ships—see which one gets to the water-wheel first."

"Yes, I'll do that," agreed Janet.

At the lower end of the brook she and Teddy had built a little dam, and where the water flowed over the top, like a tiny Niagara Falls, Teddy had fastened a wooden paddle wheel which turned as the water flowed on it.

"Me want a s'ip!" wailed Trouble, as he saw his brother and sister getting their vessels ready for the race.

"Can't you give him a piece of board for his ship, Ted?" asked Janet. "If we don't he'll get in our way and spoil the race."

"Here, Trouble, take this," and Teddy paused long enough in his work of loading pebbles on his ship to toss his little brother a small chip he picked up off the shore.

"Hu! I want bigger s'ip 'n' *him*!" declared Trouble, with a grunt. Then he arose and toddled off through the bushes. Teddy and Janet were so busy getting their own vessels ready for the coming race that they paid no more attention to their small brother. And Trouble was going to get into trouble—you may be sure of that.

Howard R. Garis

"Don't put too many stones on your ship, Jan," called Ted to his sister, as he saw that she was piling on the pebbles.

"Why not?" she asked.

"'Cause you'll make it so heavy that it won't sail fast. Course I want to beat you," Ted went on, "but I want to beat you *fair*."

"Oh, thank you," Janet answered. "But these aren't stones I'm loading on my ship this time."

"What are they?" asked Ted.

"Feathers," his sister answered. "I'm making believe the stones are feathers, and I'm going to sell them to make pillows for dolls. My ship won't be too heavy!"

"Hu!" grunted Ted, as he placed the pebbles carefully on the middle of his ship, so it would not turn over. "Stones are heavy, whether you make believe they're feathers or not. Don't put too many on, I'm telling you!"

"All right, I won't," agreed Janet.

The boy and the girl went on with their game, and they were almost ready to start their ships off on the race when there was a racket in the bushes back of them. It was a bumping, banging sound that Ted and Janet heard, then followed the bark of a dog.

"That's Skyrocket!" said Ted.

A moment later came a voice, calling:

"Whoa-up! Don't go so fas'! You is spillin' me!"

"That's Trouble!" declared Janet.

They were both right. A moment later there burst through the bushes the little boy and the dog. The dog was Skyrocket, and he was made fast to a box which he was dragging along by a rope tied around his neck. Trouble was holding to the rear of the box, and in his eagerness to pull it along Skyrocket was also dragging Trouble, "spillin'" him, in fact—that is, pulling Trouble off his feet every now and then.

"Why, William! what are you doing?" asked Janet. Trouble was hardly ever called by his right name of William unless he had done something wrong.

"Were you trying to have Skyrocket ride you in that box?" asked Teddy. "If you were, he can't. Sky can't pull you in that box unless it has wheels on it. Then it's a wagon."

"Don't want wagon—dis my s'ip!" announced the little fellow, as he began to loosen the rope from the dog's neck. But as soon as Trouble started to do this, Skyrocket, who loved the children, began to lick William's face with a red tongue.

"'Top it! 'Top it!" commanded Trouble, but Skyrocket only licked the more.

"Oh, Ted, unfasten Sky, or he'll eat Trouble up!" laughed Janet.

"Are you going to sail that big box for your ship, Trouble?" asked Ted, as he loosed the dog.

"Yep! Dis box my s'ip," announced the small boy. "I sail it!"

"Well, don't sail it near ours or you'll upset our ships—yours

Howard R. Garis

is so much larger, dear," begged Janet.

"I be ca'eful!" Trouble promised. "I find this big box for my s'ip in kitchen, an' Sky drag it here for me!"

"Yes, Skyrocket is a good dog," said Ted. "Hi there! Don't wag your tail so near my ship, or you'll upset her before I beat Jan in the race!" shouted Teddy, as the dog, in his joy at being with the Curlytops, nearly spoiled their plans for having fun.

"Here! Go chase that!" cried Ted, tossing a stick far down the brook. And as Skyrocket splashed into the water after it, a loud whistle was heard across the field on the other side of the brook.

"There's the postman!" called Janet.

"Yes, he's coming here, and he's got a letter in his hand," announced Teddy. "He's taking the short cut."

Sometimes the mail carrier came across the lots near the Martin home, as he was doing on this occasion. The Curlytops ceased the loading of their ships long enough to run and meet the carrier.

"There's a letter for your mother," the postman said, as he handed the missive to Ted. "Don't drop it in the brook."

"I won't," promised the boy. "I wonder who the letter is from?" he went on, as the postman continued over the lots to his next stopping place, blowing his whistle on the way.

"Any mail, children?" called a voice.

"There's mother, now!" said Janet.

"Yes, here's a letter," called Ted. His mother had walked down to the brook from the house, along the back path, to see what her Curlytops and Trouble were doing.

Mrs. Martin opened and read the letter as Ted and Janet went back to their play, and as she turned the pages she gave an exclamation of wonder.

"What is it?" asked Ted, looking up as he placed the last pebble on his ship.

"This is a letter from your Uncle Toby," said Mrs. Martin, "and there is strange news in it. I wonder what it means? This is very queer!"

She started to read the letter again, but at that moment Janet cried:

"Oh, look at Trouble! Just look at him! He's sailing away down the brook! Oh, he'll be drowned!"

Howard R. Garis

CHAPTER II

AN AUTOMOBILE RIDE

Mrs. Martin dropped the letter from Uncle Toby. It fluttered to the ground as she hastened down the bank of the brook in which Trouble was sailing away, aboard the small box he had brought to play with as his "s'ip."

"William! William Anthony Martin! Come right back here!" called Mrs. Martin. "Come back!"

Poor William would have been glad enough to do this, but he could not. He had stepped into the box, shoved it out from shore with a pole as he had seen Janet poling her tiny ship along, and then the current of the stream had carried poor Trouble away. He was floating down the brook, which was quite deep in some places.

"Oh, Trouble! Trouble! What shall I do?" cried his mother.

"I'll run up to the house and get the rake, and we can hook it on the edge of his box and pull him out!" shouted Janet.

"I'll get him myself!" called Ted, and, not thinking that he had on his shoes and stockings, into the water he dashed, following after the floating box in which Trouble was riding.

As for the little fellow himself, he had been overjoyed, at first, when he found that he was afloat. But as the water came leaking through the cracks in the box Trouble became frightened.

"Oh, Momsie! Come an' det me! Come an' det me!" he wailed.

"Mother's coming!" called Mrs. Martin, as she caught up a long stick and, running along the edge of the brook, tried to reach out and hook it over the side of the box-ship in which William was sailing away.

And while the mother, brother and sister of the little chap are going to his rescue, I will take just a moment or two and tell you something about the Martin children, and why they are called the "Curlytops."

The reason for the odd, pretty name is not hard to find. It was in their hair—they had the cutest, curliest curly hair that ever grew on the heads of any children anywhere in the world. So it is no wonder they were called "Curlytops."

Some of you were introduced to them in the first book of this series, "The Curlytops at Cherry Farm," which told of their adventures in the country.

After that they had more adventures on "Star Island," where they went camping with Grandpa. The fun on the island was wonderful, even more wonderful were their adventures when they were "Snowed In" and when the Curlytops went to Uncle Frank's ranch, and rode on ponyback. Ted, Janet and Trouble thought they had never seen such good times in all their lives. They helped solve a strange mystery, too.

The book just before this one that you are reading is named

"The Curlytops at Silver Lake," and in that you may learn what Ted, Janet and Trouble did when they went on the water with Uncle Ben, and how they helped capture some bad men.

The summer had been filled with adventures, and there were some good times in the winter that followed. Now it was summer again, and the Curlytops were ready for more fun.

Mr. Richard Martin was the father of the Curlytops. He was a storekeeper in the city of Cresco, in one of our eastern states. There were just three of the Curlytops, Theodore Baradale, Janet and William Anthony Martin. But Theodore was nearly always called Ted or Teddy, Janet's name was shortened to Jan and William answered to the call of Trouble as often as to any other.

In addition to the children there was Skyrocket, the dog, and Turnover, the cat. The cat was called that name because she had a trick of lying down and rolling over when she wanted something to eat. There had also been Nicknack, a goat, and Clipclap, a pony, but these had been sent away for a time, and the dog and cat were the only pets the children had at present. But they were soon going to have more, as I will tell you presently.

It was a warm, pleasant, sunny day when Ted and Jan went down to the brook to play that pieces of boards were their "ships." Then Trouble had joined them, and, just after the mail carrier left the strange letter from Uncle Toby, Trouble had, as usual, gotten into trouble.

Janet and Teddy were not quite certain who Uncle Toby might be. They had heard of him, once or twice, as a distant relative of their father or their mother, but they had not seen him in a number of years. They only dimly remembered him as an old man who lived in a city about fifty miles from Cresco, but they had not visited him in some time.

Just now the plight of Trouble so filled the minds of Ted and Jan that they had no thought for Uncle Toby or his strange letter. Nor did Mrs. Martin give any heed to the missive she had dropped.

"Be careful, Teddy!" she called, as she saw her older son splashing his way through the water. "Don't fall!"

"I—I won't, Mother! Not if—if I—I can help—"

But just as Teddy got that far he stumbled on a round stone in the brook, and down he went with a splash!

"Oh, he'll be drowned!" screamed Janet, who was following her mother along the bank of the brook, while Trouble was out in the middle in his leaking, packing-box ship that Skyrocket had pulled to the stream for him. The dog, who had found the stick which Teddy threw, had rushed back, and was now barking as loudly as he could.

But the water was not deep enough to drown Teddy. It, however, made him very wet. Up he rose, dripping all over, and gasping for breath.

Mrs. Martin paused only long enough to look back and see that Teddy was all right, and then hurried along, trying to pull toward her, with the long stick, the floating box and her little son.

"Det me out! Det me out! I is all wet—I is!" cried Trouble. "My hoots is all wet!" Sometimes the letter "f" bothered him, and he put an "h" in its place, as saying "hoots" for "foots." Of course neither word was right, but who minded a thing

Howard R. Garis

like that when poor Trouble was in such a plight?

"I'll get him!" cried Teddy, as he caught his breath. Then he wiped some of the water from his face, and dashed on down the brook. But by this time the packing box, in which Trouble was taking more of a ride than he had counted on, was some distance down the brook. However, Mrs. Martin was keeping alongside of it, though it was beyond even the reach of her long stick.

"If we were on the other side you could reach him and pull him to shore, Mother!" called Janet.

"Oh, I must get over on the other side—but the brook is deep here!" said Mrs. Martin. She was going to forget that, however, and splash in, when the box, by some twist of the current, suddenly floated near the bank along which she was running.

"Grab it—quick!" cried Janet.

"Let me get it—I'm coming!" shouted Teddy, and, indeed, he was splashing his way down the brook, but some distance behind his little brother.

"Oh, det me out! My hoots is awful wet!" wailed the small chap in the packing-box boat.

And just then Mrs. Martin was able to reach out her stick, hook one end of it over the edge of the box and pull it to shore.

"You poor little fellow! Was mother's Trouble frightened to pieces?" murmured Mrs. Martin as she lifted her youngest out of the box, and, never minding his wet feet, hugged him tightly. The packing box drifted off downstream, Skyrocket racing after it and barking as though it was the best joke in the world. "Were you frightened, William?" murmured his mother.

Trouble looked at her, and then at the floating box.

"I had a nice wide, but my hoots is all wet," he announced.

"I should say they were!" laughed Janet, feeling them. "They're soaking wet! But you're all right now, Trouble!"

"And I'm wet, too," said Teddy, coming along just then.

Together they walked back along the edge of the brook, Skyrocket following when he found that no one was going to help him play with the empty box, which floated ashore near the dam Teddy had made.

As she passed the place where she had dropped Uncle Toby's letter Mrs. Martin picked up the fluttering paper.

"I nearly forgot all about this," she said. "Your father will want to know about it. I never heard anything so strange in all my life."

"What is it?" asked Teddy.

"I'll tell you when you have dry clothes on, and we can sit down and talk it over," his mother promised.

And when Trouble, smiling and happy, with a picture book in his hands and dry shoes and stockings on his feet, was safe in a chair, and when Janet and Teddy sat near her, Mrs. Martin read the letter again.

"It is from Uncle Toby Bardeen of Pocono," said the mother

of the Curlytops. "At least he is your father's uncle, but that doesn't matter. He is an old bachelor, and lives with a distant relative, a Mrs. Watson, in an old, rambling house."

"Does he want us to come there for the summer vacation?" asked Janet. It was time, so she and Ted thought, to begin thinking of the summer fun.

"No, Uncle Toby doesn't say that," went on Mother Martin, as she glanced over the pages of the letter. "What he wants is for your father to go and take charge of everything that is in the old house—everything, that is, except the housekeeper, Mrs. Watson. She is going off by herself, Uncle Toby says."

"Is Uncle Toby—is he—dead, that he wants daddy to take everything in his house?" asked Janet.

"Course not! How could he be dead and write this letter?" asked Ted.

"Well, maybe he wrote it before he died," Janet suggested.

"No, Uncle Toby isn't dead, I'm glad to say," remarked Mrs. Martin. "But he is going away on a long voyage for his health, he writes, and he wants daddy to come and take charge of everything in the old mansion."

"Do you s'pose there's a gun there I could have?" asked Teddy hopefully.

"I'd like an old-fashioned spinning wheel," said Janet. "Is there one of those, Mother?"

"I wants suffin' to eat!" announced Trouble suddenly, but whether he thought it was to be had at Uncle Toby's house or not, it is hard to say.

Teddy and Janet laughed, and Trouble looked at them with wondering eyes.

"You shall have something to eat, love!" his mother murmured. "I guess your voyage in the packing-box ship made you hungry."

"Do you s'pose Uncle Toby would have a gun?" asked Ted again.

"If there is one in his house *you* can't have it, my dear," objected Mrs. Martin.

"But I could have the spinning wheel, couldn't I?" asked Janet.

"Yes, I suppose so. But maybe there isn't one," her mother answered.

"If there is we can play steamboat!" cried Ted, getting quickly over his disappointment about a possible gun. "A spinning wheel is just the thing to steer a make-believe steamer with!"

"You're not going to have my spinning wheel for your old steamboat!" declared Janet.

"Hush, children!" their mother warned them. "I haven't the least idea what is in Uncle Toby's house, that he should be so mysterious about it, and be in such a hurry for your father to come and take charge."

"Is Uncle Toby mysterious?" asked Janet.

"Well, yes. He says he hopes the collection will not be too much for us to manage," went on Mrs. Martin, with another look at the letter.

"A collection of what?" Ted wanted to know.

"That's just it—Uncle Toby doesn't say," his mother replied. "We shall have to wait until your father makes the trip to Pocono."

"Oh, may we go?" begged the two Curlytops at once.

"We'll see!" was the way in which Mrs. Martin put them off. "I wish your father were here so we could talk over this queer letter from Uncle Toby."

"I wis'—I wis' I had suffin' t' *eat*!" put in Trouble wistfully.

"And so you shall have, darling!" exclaimed his mother. "It is nearly time for lunch, and daddy will soon be here. Then we'll see what he says."

And what Mr. Martin said after, at the lunch table, he had read Uncle Toby's letter was:

"Hum!"

"What do you think of it?" asked his wife.

"I think it's as queer as he is," said the father of the Curlytops, smiling. "Uncle Toby is a dear old man, but very queer. So he wants me to come and take charge of his 'collection,' does he? It's strange that he doesn't say what his collection is."

"Maybe it's postage stamps," suggested Ted. Once he had started to make a collection like that but he had given it up.

"And maybe it's a collection of—money!" said Janet.

"That would be very fine!" laughed her father. "But though Uncle Toby is well off, I hardly think he has a collection of money lying around his old mansion. However, I suppose I must go and see what it is the queer fellow wants me to take charge of for him."

"May we go?" chorused Ted and Janet again.

"Oh, I suppose so," agreed their father, and this was better than the "I'll see," of their mother.

"Me tum too!" declared Trouble. He never wanted to be left behind.

"We'll all take an auto trip over to Pocono to-morrow and see what Uncle Toby has," decided Mr. Martin.

Accordingly, the next day, Mr. Martin left his manager in charge of the store, and, in the comfortable family automobile, the Curlytops and their father, mother and Trouble— not forgetting Skyrocket, the dog—started off.

It was just as fine a day as the previous one, when Trouble had sailed down the brook. The grass was green, the birds sang, and the wind blew gently in the trees.

"Oh, it's summer, and there's no school and well have lots of fun!" sang Janet.

"Maybe we'll have fun with what we find at Uncle Toby's house," suggested Ted.

And neither of the Curlytops realized how much fun nor what strange adventures were in store for them.

The automobile started down a rather steep hill, and Mrs. Martin, who was on the front seat with her husband, looked back to see that the three children were safe.

"Hold on to Trouble!" she told Janet. "He might bounce out. The road is very rough!"

"Yes, it isn't very safe, either," murmured Mr. Martin. "I hope nothing happens."

Hardly had he spoken than there was a loud bang close behind him. He jammed on the brakes and cried:

"Tire's burst! Hold tight—everybody!"

Then the automobile slid over to one side of the road and Janet cried:

"Oh, Trouble! Trouble!"

CHAPTER III

THE QUEER OLD LADY

For a little while it seemed as though something serious had happened in the automobile which was taking the Curlytops to Uncle Toby's house. Mr. Martin had all he could do to slow up the machine, bringing it to a stop beside the road, and under a tree. If a tire had burst or been punctured Daddy Martin wanted to be in the shade to fix it.

Mother Martin, holding tightly to the side of the seat when the banging noise sounded, turned to look behind her to see if the three children were all right. She saw Trouble sitting between Ted and Janet, and William was looking at something in his chubby hand.

"What happened?" asked Mrs. Martin. "Were any of you hurt when the tire burst?"

"The tire didn't burst, Mother," answered Teddy.

"Why, I heard it," said Mr. Martin, as he prepared to get out of the machine, which had now come to a stop. "I must have run over a sharp stone or a broken bottle."

"No, it wasn't the tire," said Janet, and she laughed. "It was

Trouble's toy balloon. He blew it up too big and it burst."

"That's what it was! And a piece of the rubber hit me in the eye!" laughed Ted.

"My 'loon all gone!" wailed William.

"So that's what it was—a burst toy balloon," said Daddy Martin. "Well, I'm glad it wasn't one of my tires."

"So am I," said Mother Martin. "It is too hot to have to change a tire to-day. Besides, I'm in a hurry to get to Uncle Toby's and see what it is he wants us to take charge of while he is away. I hope he doesn't go until we get there."

"You never can tell what Uncle Toby is going to do," said Mr. Martin, smiling, now that he knew he had no tire to change. "And so you burst your toy balloon, did you, Trouble? Well, I'll have to get you another, but not while we're on this auto ride. I don't want to be frightened again, and I might be if you blew up another balloon and it burst."

"I didn't know he had one with him," remarked Mrs. Martin, as Trouble looked sadly at what was left of his toy.

"I didn't either," Janet said. "All of a sudden he took it out of his pocket and began to blow it up."

"I was makin' be'eve it were a wed soap bubbles," explained Trouble.

"Well, soap bubbles or not, it burst," said Teddy. "It sure did make a noise! But now we can go on. I want to see if Uncle Toby is going to leave any guns."

"And I want a spinning wheel," Janet murmured. "But you

can't take it to play steamboat with," she told her brother.

"I shan't want it if I have a gun!" retorted Ted.

"Now, children, be nice," begged their mother.

Daddy Martin started the automobile again, first getting out to look at the four tires, to make sure none was flat, punctured or burst. They were all round, plump and as fat as big bologna sausages.

"Now we go to Uncle Toby. Maybe I get a kittie cat!" said Trouble, when he decided to smile after feeling so bad about his burst balloon.

"A kittie cat!" exclaimed Janet. "Why, we have a lovely cat, Trouble. Don't you like Turnover?"

"Yep! But I 'ikes a kittie cat, too. Maybe Uncle Toby hab one for me!"

"Probably Uncle Toby is too old a man to bother with pet cats," said Mrs. Martin.

But it only goes to show that you never know what is going to happen in this world—sometimes you don't even know what you are going to have for dinner.

Along rolled the automobile, taking the Curlytops nearer and nearer to the city of Pocono, where Uncle Toby lived with his housekeeper, Mrs. Watson. But it was rather a long ride, and, about half way, the party stopped in a little village for lunch.

"Did we bring any lunch with us, or are we going in a place to eat?" asked Ted.

Howard R. Garis

"Oh, I hope we go in a place to eat!" exclaimed Janet. "I like a restaurant, don't you, Ted?"

"Sure!" answered the Curlytop boy.

"Yes, we are going to a restaurant," his mother told them. "Daddy wants to get some oil and gasoline for the auto, too."

"It's sort of feeding the auto, isn't it, Mother?" asked Janet, as they alighted.

"In a way, yes," admitted Mrs. Martin.

A little later the Curlytops were having a fine meal, and when I say the Curlytops I mean also Daddy and Mother Martin, and Trouble. The hair of Mr. and Mrs. Martin did not curl, though it must have done so when they were younger; or else how would Ted and Janet have had such beautiful ringlets? Nor did Trouble's hair curl, though when he was smaller his mother used to wind little ringlets around her finger, hoping he would have locks as pretty as those of Janet and Ted. But, really, the older boy and girl were the only ones who could, truly, be called Curlytops, though I sometimes speak of the "Curlytop family."

So you know, when I say that the "Curlytops" were eating lunch, that all five of them were enjoying their meal. There were several things that Janet, Teddy and Trouble liked to eat, and toward the end of the meal there was a piece of pie for each of them. And it was toward the end of the meal that something happened, and Trouble, as usual, was the cause of it.

Just before the waiter had brought the pie there had sounded, out in the street, the music of a hand organ. No sooner had he heard this than Trouble slipped from his chair (where he had been sitting on a hassock to make him higher) and ran to the window.

"No monkey!" called out the little fellow, after he had stood for a moment with his nose pressed against the pane of glass, making his "smeller," as he sometimes called it, quite flat. "Hand-organ grinder got no monkey!"

Trouble was disappointed. He had hoped to see a little monkey scrambling around to gather pennies in his cap. But this hand-organ player did not have any. And there was nothing much for Trouble to see. So the little fellow came back to the table, but not before he had stopped at the big water-cooler in one corner of the dining room. Trouble paused to watch a waiter turn the shiny little faucet and draw a glass of water for a customer.

"Come and get your pie, William," his mother called to him. She very seldom mentioned him as "Trouble," before strangers. So this time Mrs. Martin called her little boy by his right name.

"Do you want me to eat your pie?" teased Ted.

"No! I eat my own pie!" Trouble exclaimed, and he climbed up into his chair, being helped by his father, next to whom he sat.

The meal was almost over, and Daddy Martin was wondering what his Uncle Toby could want him to take charge of, when Mrs. Martin gave a sudden start, a sort of shiver, and said:

"Why, my feet are getting wet!"

"Your feet wet!" exclaimed her husband. "Surely it isn't

Howard R. Garis

raining in here! It isn't even raining outside!" he laughed, as he looked from a window.

"But my feet are damp," went on Mrs. Martin. Then she raised the cloth, which hung down rather low on each side of the table, and glanced at the floor. "There's a big puddle of water under our table!" she cried.

Then Ted looked over toward the big water-cooler in one corner of the restaurant.

"Somebody left the faucet open!" cried Teddy. "The ice water is all running out! No wonder your feet are wet, Mother!"

Mr. Martin hastily left his chair and turned off the faucet, and, as he did so, he looked at Trouble. Something in the face of that youngster caused Daddy Martin to ask:

"William, did you do that?"

"I—I dess maybe I turned it on a 'ittle bit!" confessed the mischievous one.

"A *little* bit!" cried Janet, as she looked under the table. "Why, there's almost as much water as there is in our brook at home!"

"Oh, not quite so much," said her mother gently. "Though there is enough to have wet through the soles of my shoes. I was wondering why my feet felt so damp and cold. And did Trouble turn on the water? Oh, Trouble!"

All eyes gazed at the little fellow, and he seemed to think he should explain what he had done.

"I 'ist turned de handle a teeny bit," he said, "to make a 'ittle water come out. An' den I fordot 'bout it!"

That was just what he had done. Seeing the waiter draw a glass of water from the cooler had given Trouble the idea that he soon afterward carried out. When he saw no monkey with the hand organ, the little fellow had gone back to his seat and, on the way, opened the faucet so that the water ran out in a little stream. Soon the drip-pan was full and then the water began trickling over the floor. No one noticed it until it had made a little puddle under the table, just at the point where Mrs. Martin's feet were.

"Oh, Trouble! what will you do next?" sighed the little fellow's mother.

"No harm done at all! None whatever!" said the waiter, coming up to the table smiling. "That little water on the floor I will wipe up so quick you will never see it."

"No, it won't hurt the floor much," Mr. Martin said. "And I suppose your shoes will dry out," he told his wife. "But, all the same, William should not have done it."

"I won't do it any more," said the little fellow. "I be good now! I sorry!"

He generally was when he had done something like that. However, as the waiter had said, little real harm was done, and Mrs. Martin's shoes would dry, for it was a hot, summer day.

The meal was finished and they all took their places in the automobile again to finish the ride to Uncle Toby's place, about twenty miles farther on.

Once again Trouble, Ted and Janet sat in the rear seat, while their father and mother rode in front. And this time Trouble had no red balloon which he could blow up, making it burst with a noise like a punctured tire. The children talked among themselves, wondering over and over again what it could be that Uncle Toby wanted their father to come and take charge of.

"Maybe he's got a little boy or a girl from an orphan asylum, and he wants us to take it to live with us," suggested Janet.

"A boy would be all right," decided Ted, as he thought of this. "I could have fun with another fellow."

"And I'd like a girl," said Janet. "I always wished I had a sister."

"Maybe they're twins—a boy and a girl," Ted went on. "That would be fun!"

"What would be fun?" asked his mother from the front seat, where she had heard the talk of the children. She often asked a question like this, as it sometimes stopped a bit of mischief that, otherwise, might happen. "What fun are you talking about?" asked Mrs. Martin.

"Uncle Toby," answered Janet. "I thought maybe what he wanted daddy to take charge of was a little orphan girl."

"And I thought maybe it was a boy," added Ted.

"And then we both thought maybe it was twins—a boy and a girl, and we'd each have someone to play with," went on Janet.

"My! I don't believe Uncle Toby has adopted any orphan

children that he wants us to take," Mrs. Martin said. "I can't imagine what he really has, but we'll soon find out."

On and on they rode in the automobile, until, after a while, they reached the small city of Pocono and, a little later, they pulled up in front of Uncle Toby's house. It was a rambling, old mansion that once had looked very nice, but now it was rather shabby and needed painting.

"Here is where Uncle Toby lives," said Daddy Martin. "Do you children remember it?"

"A little," admitted Ted. Neither he nor Janet had been there in years, and Trouble had never visited Uncle Toby.

"I wonder if he's at home," went on Daddy Martin, as he alighted from the automobile.

"There's someone on the porch," said Mrs. Martin. "Oh, it's Mrs. Watson, the housekeeper," she added. "But something seems to be the matter! I wonder what can have happened?"

As Mother Martin spoke a queer little old lady came down off the porch and along the walk, hurrying out to meet the Curlytops, all of whom were now at the front gate.

"Wait! Don't go in! Don't go in!" cried the queer old lady, holding up her hand like a traffic policeman stopping a fast automobile. "Don't go in! They're having a terrible time! Oh, that Mr. Bardeen ever should have gone away and left me to look after 'em! Oh, the trouble I have had! Such trouble! Don't go in! Listen to 'em!"

As she spoke there came strange sounds from the grim old house where Uncle Toby lived! Very strange sounds!

Howard R. Garis

CHAPTER IV

UNCLE TOBY'S PETS

"Listen to that noise!" called Teddy, pausing with his hand on the gate that led into Uncle Toby's yard. "It's two boys having fun. I guess Uncle Toby left two fellows that you can take home and I can have fun with," Teddy added laughingly to his father.

"Two boys! Oh, my goodness!" exclaimed Mrs. Martin.

Just then a shrill scream sounded from within the queer, old house.

"It's girls!" said Janet. "Girls cry just like that when they're having fun! Oh, I'll be glad to have a sister to play with!"

Mr. and Mrs. Martin looked at each other in surprise and wonderment. What could it mean? The queer, little old lady—Mrs. Watson, the housekeeper—murmured again:

"Listen to 'em! I can't do a thing with 'em since Uncle Toby went away. I'm so glad you came to take charge of 'em as he asked you to. You did come for that, didn't you?" she asked eagerly. "You got Uncle Toby's letter, asking you to come and take charge of the collection he left, didn't you?"

"Oh, yes," answered the father of the Curlytops. "We got Uncle Toby's letter all right, and we came to take charge. But—"

"We'd like to know *what* we are going to take!" interrupted Mrs. Martin. She felt she must say something, with all those queer noises going on in the house.

"Maybe it's babies!" suggested Trouble, as he listened to what seemed to be a crying sound from the old mansion.

"They're worse than babies!" declared Mrs. Watson. "I don't mind children and babies. But these things make so much noise I can't hear myself think. That's why I came out on the steps to sit down and be quiet! Oh, I'm so glad you've come to take charge of 'em!"

"But what are they? You haven't told us what they are," said Mr. Martin, as the screeching, yelling noises kept on sounding from within the house. "Do they always screech like that?"

"Only when they're hungry," said the queer old lady. "And I expect they're hungry now. I just hate to go in to feed them, they make such a fuss, and I'm afraid some of 'em will bite me. Not on purpose you know," she quickly added, "but just because they're so playful and full of fun."

"My dear Mrs. Watson," said Mr. Martin in slow tones, "will you *please* tell us what it is my Uncle Toby has left for me to take charge of! Is it an insane asylum?"

"Yes, for goodness' sake, please tell us!" begged the mother of the Curlytops.

"Why, I thought you knew!" replied Mrs. Watson, in some

surprise. "Didn't Uncle Toby speak of them in his letter?"

"No, he did not say what they were," answered Mr. Martin. "He only mentioned a collection. Please tell us. What is making all that racket?"

"Uncle Toby's pets," was the answer. "Uncle Toby said he was going to leave them to you when he went away on a long trip. He may be gone for several years, and he said he might live the rest of his life in South America, where he is going. So he told me to give you his pets to take charge of. You are to take them, and do as you please with them, though I guess Uncle Toby would like to have you keep them and be kind to them."

"Uncle Toby's *pets*!" exclaimed Mrs. Martin.

"Is there a dog?" asked Teddy, his eyes shining in delight. "Won't Skyrocket be glad? Do you hear that, old fellow?" went on Teddy, leaning down to pet the dog that had jumped from the automobile and was looking as if in wonder at the house whence came such strange noises. "You're going to have another dog to play with. Uncle Toby did leave a dog, didn't he?" Teddy asked of Mrs. Watson. "I hear a dog barking in the house."

"A dog!" exclaimed the queer little old housekeeper. "He left *two* dogs, Uncle Toby did!"

"Two dogs!" murmured Mrs. Martin, with a hopeless look at her husband.

"Did he leave a cat?" asked Janet. "I thought I heard one mewing. And Turnover would like another cat to play with."

"Yes, Uncle Toby left you a cat, also," said Mrs. Watson.

Just then shrill screams, barks, squeaks and squawks, all mixed together, seemed to float out of the opened windows of the old house—windows in which were strong wire screens.

"Two dogs and a cat!" exclaimed Mr. Martin. "My dear Mrs. Watson," he went on, as he sat down on the top step of the porch rather limply, "will you please tell us, as fast as you can, just how many and what pets Uncle Toby has left us? We may as well hear the worst at once," he said to his wife. "I never imagined Uncle Toby cared for animal pets."

"Oh, indeed he did," replied Mrs. Watson. "Of late years he grew very fond of animals. All his pets are animals, and he'd have gotten more only I said I wouldn't stay and keep house for him if he brought in what he spoke of last."

"What was that?" Mrs. Martin wanted to know.

"*Snakes*!" declared the little old lady. "I don't mind monkeys and parrots so much, but I can't bear *snakes*! They give me the shivers, though Uncle Toby said some snakes do a lot of good in this world, by catching rats and mice. But he didn't bring in any snakes!"

"Do you mean to say he has a parrot?" asked Mr. Martin.

"Don't you hear him?" questioned Mrs. Watson. "Listen!"

As she finished speaking the Curlytops heard a shrill:

"Cracker! Cracker! Give Polly a crack-crack-cracker!"

"Oh, it *is* a parrot!" cried Janet in delight.

"And is there a monkey, too?" demanded Ted.

"An' a han' ordan! Is dere a han' ordan?" asked Trouble.

"No hand organ, child, no," answered Mrs. Watson. "But there is a monkey, a parrot, two dogs, and a cat, a—"

"Stop! Wait a moment!" begged Mrs. Martin. She took a seat beside her husband on the top step. "I just wanted to sit down before I fainted when I heard the worst," she went on. "Now go ahead, Mrs. Watson. Tell me the rest. I'll have something to lean against in case she tells me there's an elephant."

"An elephant!" cried Janet.

"Oh, I don't mean I want to lean on the elephant," said her mother. "I just want to lean against the piazza post. This is the worst I ever heard of—Uncle Toby leaving us a menagerie!"

"'Tisn't quite as bad as that, though 'tis, almost," said Mrs. Watson. "There isn't an elephant, but there is an alligator."

"An alligator! Oh, that's great!" cried Ted. "Where is it?"

"This is terrible!" declared his mother.

"It's only a little alligator," explained the housekeeper. "He's real friendly, though his tail scratches when he rubs it against your hand as you feed him."

"Anything else?" asked Mr. Martin. "Please go on. We may as well hear the worst. It sounds like a circus that Uncle Toby kept in his house. What else, Mrs. Watson?"

"Well? that's about all, except some white rats and mice and the pigeons. Uncle Toby didn't get the snake he wanted."

"Let us be thankful for that," murmured Mrs. Martin, "though it is bad enough as it is."

"Bad?" cried Teddy. "I think it's jolly! Can't we go in and see Uncle Toby's pets?" he asked.

"They're going to be our pets, aren't they, Daddy?" asked Jan. "Didn't Uncle Toby say you could have them?"

"That's what he said," replied the father of the Curlytops. "But I don't know whether to take him at his word or not. But we may as well go in and look at the—the menagerie!" he said to his wife, with a smile.

"They'll need feeding—the animals will," said Mrs. Watson. "I'm glad you're here to help me. I was staying only until you came. Uncle Toby said you'd be over in a day or two. I'm leaving to-night, now you're here."

"What? And make us take care of all the pets?" cried Mrs. Martin.

"Oh, they're real kind and gentle—every one, even the little alligator," Uncle Toby's housekeeper made haste to say. "And as long as you have children the pets will be just the things for the Curlytops. Only I can't stay much longer. I was just waiting for you. I went outside as it was quieter," she concluded, as, once again, the pet animals set up a screeching, barking and mewing.

"Well, let's get it over with," suggested Mr. Martin. "Maybe they'll be quieter if we feed them. Is there anything in the house for the menagerie to eat?" he asked the little old housekeeper.

"Oh, yes, Uncle Toby always fed them well," she answered.

"Oh, I'm so glad you came to take charge of the pets!"

"I don't know whether we are or not," remarked Mrs. Martin. "I suppose, though," she said to her husband in a low voice, as they prepared to enter the house, "we can sell them. We don't have to keep them."

"Yes, I guess that would be best—to sell them," agreed Mr. Martin, but he did not let the Curlytops hear him say this.

Led by Mrs. Watson, the Curlytop party entered the house. As the door was opened the different noises sounded more loudly than before.

The dogs barked—and Ted could now hear the tones of two different animals—the cat mewed, the monkey screeched and chattered, and the parrot cried:

"Give Polly a cracker! Polly wants a crack-crack-cracker!"

"I guess the alligator is the only one that isn't saying anything," remarked Mr. Martin to his wife as they entered. "And I never heard that alligators make a noise."

"Yes they do!" said Janet, eagerly. "I read it in my natural history book. They make a noise like a grunt. At least it's either alligators or crocodiles, I've forgotten which. But one kind bellows like a bull."

"Goodness! Let us hope this one doesn't!" sighed Mrs. Martin. "Who would ever think that Uncle Toby would keep a menagerie!" she murmured.

"I never did," agreed her husband.

"They're all in one big room—a sort of addition to the house.

It opens off the dining room," explained Mrs. Watson. "Uncle Toby liked to eat when his pets did, that's why he had 'em so near him in the dining room. I'll show 'em to you."

"Are the pigeons out there, too?" asked Mrs. Martin.

"No, Uncle Toby kept them in the barn," the housekeeper replied. "If you don't want the pigeons, Uncle Toby told me to tell you there's a boy in this same street who will take them. But Uncle Toby said he wished you'd take charge of all the other pets."

"Oh, yes, Mother—Daddy! Let's keep 'em *all*!" pleaded Janet.

By this time Mrs. Watson had opened the door leading into the extra room that Uncle Toby had built to house his pets. No sooner was the door opened than the noise sounded louder than ever, and several things happened.

"Oh, look at the lovely cat!" cried Janet, as one with very fluffy fur walked forward as though to meet the Curlytops. "It's a Persian, I guess. Oh, I just love a Persian! Turnover is very nice, but I love this one a lot," and she reached down to stroke the beautiful cat that seemed very friendly.

"Oh, look!" suddenly cried Ted. "See! The dogs do tricks!"

As he spoke one white poodle came walking along on his hind legs, with his front paws held in a funny fashion before him.

"Bow wow!" barked the poodle. And then, as if this might be a signal, there suddenly came from the end of the room another white poodle, so nearly like the first that it was difficult to tell them apart.

"Oh, see! More tricks!" cried Ted.

The second dog began turning somersaults. One after another he turned, making his way, in this fashion, to where Ted was patting the head of the poodle that was standing on its hind legs.

"Say! I can have a regular circus with these trick dogs!" cried Ted in delight.

"And my Persian cat can be in it," added Janet.

Just then a cry, as if of fear, came from Trouble. Turning around the Curlytops and others saw a strange sight.

A brown monkey was hanging by its tail from an electric chandelier in the middle of the room, and, thus reaching down, was trying to pull Trouble's cap from the little fellow's head.

"'Top! 'Top it!" shouted William. "Make han'-ordan monkey let my cap alone!" he wailed. And then, with a flutter and a screech, a green and red parrot flew from its perch and landed on Mrs. Martin's shoulder. The pets of the Curlytops were having a lively time!

CHAPTER V

TIP AND TOP

With the barking of the trick dogs, in which Skyrocket joined, and with the mewing of the Persian cat, the shrieking of the parrot, and the chattering of the monkey, for a time there was so much noise in Uncle Toby's "menagerie," as it was called, that the voices of Mr. and Mrs. Martin could scarcely be heard. But you could hear the voice of Trouble above everything.

"Take him off! Make him 'top!" cried the little fellow. For by this time the monkey, having hung down by his tail from the chandelier, and having taken off Trouble's cap, was now trying to pull the little boy's hair.

"Bad monkey! Make him go 'way!" cried Trouble.

"And I don't like this parrot!" said Mrs. Martin, though, to be sure, the bird was gentle enough. It only sat on her shoulder and shrieked:

"Crack! Crack! Cracker! I'm a cracker-acker!"

"Say, this is great!" cried Ted, as he watched the two dogs, one of which was marching around on his hind legs while the

Howard R. Garis

other was turning somersaults.

"Oh, it's terrible!" said Mrs. Martin. "Dick," she called to her husband, "can't you make that monkey stop hurting William?"

"He isn't exactly hurting him, my dear," replied Mr. Martin. "Though I fancy Trouble is a bit frightened. I was going to take that parrot off your shoulder."

"Well, look after William first. He needs it more than I."

Mr. Martin advanced toward the monkey, swinging by his tail from the chandelier, when Mrs. Watson, the house-keeper, said:

"I'll attend to him! I know how to manage Jack if I don't any of the other animals. I found a way to make him behave. Here!" she suddenly cried, catching up a feather-duster and shaking it at the long-tailed creature. "Get back to your cubby-hole, Jack!"

With a shrill chatter the monkey dropped Trouble's cap, which he was trying to make stick on his own head, and a moment later he jumped down from the chandelier and scampered into a box at the side of the room.

"That's where he belongs!" said Mrs. Watson. "He's always afraid of that feather-duster. Maybe he thinks it's a big eagle coming to bite his tail. Anyhow, show him the feather-duster whenever you want to quiet him."

"That's a good thing to know," said Mr. Martin, when it was a little quieter in the room, because Jack, the monkey, had stopped chattering. "But what shall we do about the parrot on my wife's shoulder?"

"Oh, Mr. Nip is all right. He's very gentle," said the housekeeper. "Uncle Toby named him Mr. Nip because he used to nip and bite when he first came. But Uncle Toby soon cured him of that. Mr. Nip is a nice polly."

"I'm a crack! I'm a crack! I'm a crack-crack-cracker!" shrieked the parrot, and then he flew from Mrs. Martin's shoulder to the regular perch, near the little cage of the monkey—the "cubby-hole," as Mrs. Watson called it.

"Thank goodness!" sighed the mother of the Curlytops.

"You scared, Mother?" asked Trouble, who was now wishing the monkey would come back, for after his first fright, the little fellow rather liked the fuzzy chap.

"Only a little," said Mrs. Martin, for she thought if the Curlytops were to have anything to do with Uncle Toby's pets, it would not be well for her to say they frightened her.

"I 'ike 'em all," remarked Trouble, while Janet was rubbing the big Persian cat and Ted was playing with the two dogs. "Uncle Toby nice man to have all nanimals 'ike dis!" and he looked around the room. Surely there were quite a number of animal pets there.

"How in the world did my uncle ever come to have so many?" asked Mr. Martin. "And what in the world are we going to do with them?"

"I'll tell you about it after we've fed them," said Mrs. Watson. "They'll be quieter after they're fed, and you might as well start in now to give them something to eat. If you're going to take 'em with you and keep 'em you'll have to feed 'em."

With the help of Ted and Janet, who set out food to the dogs and cat, Uncle Toby's animals were soon all being given things to eat, and this made them quiet. Then, while the children stood and watched the animals eat, Mrs. Watson took Daddy and Mother Martin into the next room and told them about Uncle Toby and the pets.

"I never knew that my uncle was so fond of animals," said Mr. Martin.

"He wasn't, when I first came here to keep house for him," explained Mrs. Watson. "But he made friends, once, with a sailor, who had the parrot. When the sailor started off on his next sea voyage, and didn't want to take Mr. Nip, the parrot, with him, Uncle Toby said the bird could stay here. I didn't much mind that, as it was rather lonesome when Uncle Toby—as I always call him—went out. So I got to liking Mr. Nip.

"Then, after a while, another sailor gave Uncle Toby Jack, the monkey. The house was more lively after that, for the monkey and parrot used to fight, though they don't any more. I thought this would be about all the pets Uncle Toby would get; but lo and behold! about a month after that another sailor, hearing that Uncle Toby had a monkey and a parrot, came and asked us if we wouldn't take Slider."

"Who is Slider?" asked Mrs. Martin. "It sounds like a pair of roller skates."

"Slider is the pet alligator. He came from Florida," explained Mrs. Watson. "Uncle Toby took him in, as he had the monkey and the parrot, and I began to wonder what would happen next."

"Did anything?" asked Daddy Martin, as he watched the

Curlytops playing in the next room with the pets.

"Oh, my land, yes!" exclaimed Mrs. Watson. "It wasn't more than two weeks after he got Slider—that's the alligator—that an old circus man came along with the two dogs, Tip and Top."

"Are those their names?" asked Mrs. Martin, watching Ted as he made one of the dogs turn somersaults.

"Yes, one of the white poodles—the one with the black spot on his tail—is named Tip," the housekeeper said. "You see the spot is on the tip of his tail."

"I can see that—yes," replied Mr. Martin from where he sat. He was wondering where all this was going to end.

"And the other dog is named Top," said the housekeeper. "He has a black spot on the top of his head."

"They are both very nice, and I like the names, too—Tip and Top," remarked Mrs. Martin. "See!" she exclaimed. "Our own dog, Skyrocket, is making friends with them."

Indeed Skyrocket, the Curlytop's dog, was doing this very thing. Perhaps he wanted to learn how to walk on his hind legs and turn somersaults, as Tip and Top could do.

"Tip and Top are two valuable dogs," said Mrs. Watson. "They were once in the circus, and it was there they learned to do their tricks, though Uncle Toby taught them others."

"Why didn't the circus man keep them if they were so valuable?" asked Mrs. Martin.

"The circus man had made friends with the sailor who gave

Uncle Toby the alligator," explained the housekeeper, "and the circus man decided to become a sailor, too. He said he didn't want to keep the dogs on a ship, so he gave them to Uncle Toby."

"And that's how the menagerie started?" asked Daddy Martin.

"That's how it started," said Mrs. Watson. "There were times when I thought it would never end. That was when a lady, who was going to travel for her health, asked Uncle Toby to keep Snuff, her Persian cat."

"Is Snuff the cat's name?" asked the mother of the Curlytops.

"Yes," answered Mrs. Watson. "It is just the color of snuff, you see, a sort of yellowish brown. Many Persian cats have that color, I'm told. Anyhow this lady—I've forgotten her name—said she saw that Uncle Toby loved animals, as he had so many of them, so she asked him to keep her cat."

"And Uncle Toby did," remarked Mrs. Martin.

"Uncle Toby surely did!" declared the housekeeper. "It seemed he couldn't say 'no' where animals were concerned. By this time the house began to be rather overrun with pets, so he built this room out of the dining room, with special cages—cubby-holes I call 'em—for the pets. I did think Snuff would be the last one, but after that came the white mice and rats."

"It's usually the other way about," said Mrs. Martin, with a smile. "When the cat comes the mice go. But this time the mice came after the cat arrived."

"Yes," agreed the housekeeper. "Snuff, the cat, and the white mice—I don't know their names—are great friends. The mice and rats belonged to a boy down the street. His family moved to another state last summer, and his folks made him get rid of the mice. He brought them to Uncle Toby, and of course Uncle Toby couldn't say no, so he kept them. It was then I first threatened to leave. The house was too full of animals."

"But you didn't go," said Mrs. Martin.

"No, I stayed on, because Uncle Toby begged me to, and he said he wouldn't add to his collection. But then came the pigeons. They were brought by another boy, whose folks moved away and he couldn't keep 'em any more. I didn't so much mind the pigeons, as they stay out in the barn. But we certainly had a houseful of pets! After a while I got rather to liking them, and Uncle Toby was very fond of 'em, and taught 'em many tricks."

"But finally, as you know from the letter he wrote you, he decided to take a long trip, and perhaps he may never come back, if he finds he likes it in South America. So he decided to ask you to take charge of his collection, and I said I'd stay until you arrived, as Uncle Toby had to leave in a hurry, to catch a ship that was sailing for South America."

"Why did he go there?" asked Mr. Martin.

"I think it was because he heard that monkeys and parrots come from there," the housekeeper answered. "He seemed to like those animals better than any others, though Tip and Top, the two dogs, are more valuable, because they can do circus tricks."

"They certainly are cute," said Mrs. Martin.

"Well, there you have the story of Uncle Toby's pets," said Mrs. Watson, "though I suppose they'll be the Curlytops' pets now, for Uncle Toby said he was going to give you his collection."

"Hum! Yes," mused Mr. Martin. "If I had known what the collection was I don't believe I would have come after it."

Mrs. Watson began putting on her hat, and from a corner of the room she picked up her valise, which she had already packed.

"Where are you going?" asked Mrs. Martin.

"I am going away," answered the housekeeper. "My plans are all made. I am going to live with my sister. All she keeps is a cat, and she puts that outside and winds the clock every night before she goes to bed. I'm going to her house. I told Uncle Toby I'd stay until the Curlytops came to take charge of the pets, and, now that you are here, I'll be going."

"But I say! Look here! What are we going to do?" asked Mr. Martin.

"Why, you're to take charge of the collection," said the housekeeper. "That's what Uncle Toby said in his letter. You are to have the pets!"

"But I don't want them! That is, we can't keep so many!" protested Daddy Martin. "Two dogs, a cat, a monkey, a parrot, an alligator and some white rats and mice, to say nothing of the pigeons! And we have a dog and cat now, and we just got rid of a goat and a pony! Oh, I say, my dear Mrs. Watson! This is too much!"

"Can't help it!" said the housekeeper as she fastened on her hat. "Uncle Toby said you were to take charge of his collection of pets. That's all I know. If he never comes back—and I don't believe he ever will—the pets are yours to keep. I'd keep them if I were you—all except the pigeons. There's a boy down the street who will take them and be glad to get 'em. The pets are valuable—especially Tip and Top, the dogs. They do tricks separately, but they do more tricks together—a sort of team, you know. Those dogs are very valuable for a show."

"Then I know what we can do," said Mr. Martin. "We can sell the pets Uncle Toby left and give the money to a home for children, or something like that. I'll do it—we'll sell the pets!"

In another moment—just as if they had been waiting for their father to say this—there came a storm of objections from Ted and Janet. In they ran from the room where they had been playing with the animals.

"Oh, don't sell 'em!" pleaded Janet.

"Let us keep 'em!" begged Ted. "Those dogs are the best I ever saw! They can do dandy tricks! I could get up a show with them and Skyrocket."

"And this cat and our other cat, too," added Janet. "Don't sell Uncle Toby's pets, Daddy! Let us keep them!"

Daddy Martin looked at his wife. And then, as if they had been waiting for something like this, Tip and Top did one of their best tricks. Tip began turning somersaults again and Top walked around on his hind legs. Then the two dogs barked, and, without anyone saying a word to them, they did another trick.

Howard R. Garis

Tip stopped turning somersaults and stood still. In an instant Top jumped up on Tip's back and stood there on his hind legs. Then Tip walked around the room.

"Oh, aren't they too sweet for anything!" cried Janet.

"That's a dandy trick!" declared Ted. "Do, please, let us keep Uncle Toby's pets for our own."

"Well," said his father slowly, "I don't see how in the world—"

But at that moment there came a knock at the door, and the dogs began to bark, the parrot shrieked, the monkey chattered and Snuff, the Persian cat, began to mew.

What was going to happen now?

CHAPTER VI

WHERE IS TIP?

"Someone is at the door," said Mrs. Martin to Uncle Toby's housekeeper.

"Yes, I hear 'em," answered the queer little old lady. "I 'spect it's the boy after the pigeons. I told him to call as soon as he saw the Curlytops arrive, and he's probably been watching for you. I'll let him in as soon as I finish putting on my hat so I can go."

But before this Mr. Martin, who was nearest the door, had opened it, and in came a boy about as old as Teddy, though without the curly locks of that little lad.

"Can I have the pigeons?" asked the new boy, taking off his cap and making a little bow to Mrs. Martin, Mrs. Watson and Daddy Martin. "Uncle Toby said I could have 'em if you folks didn't want 'em, and I've been waiting for you to come. I just saw you get here."

"Yes! Yes! Take the pigeons! Take any of the animals you want!" begged Mrs. Martin. "I don't see what in the world we are going to do with these animals!"

Howard R. Garis

"Oh, keep Tip and Top—the dogs!" begged Teddy.

"And Snuff, the cat!" added Janet.

"I 'ike monkey if he don't pull my cap off," said Trouble. "'Et's keep him!"

"And the white mice and rats wouldn't be much bother," went on Teddy.

"We never had a parrot that I can remember," cried Janet. "I could feed him, Mother."

"The alligator doesn't make much noise," Ted said.

"Dear me! We'll end up by keeping them all, I see!" laughed the father of the Curlytops. "That is, all but the pigeons," he added quickly, as he saw a look of disappointment on the face of the new boy. "You may have them, since Uncle Toby promised them to you."

"The pigeons are all I want," said the boy, whose name was Bob Nelson. "My mother won't let me have any of the other pets. And, anyhow, I have a dog and a cat. Could I get the pigeons now? I've got a basket and they are so tame I can pick 'em up. They know me. I used to help Uncle Toby feed 'em."

"Yes, you may get them," Mrs. Martin said. "We'll get rid of a few of the pets in that way. But what we are to do with the others, I'm sure I don't know."

"You'd better keep 'em," advised Mrs. Watson, who was now almost ready to go. "Uncle Toby wouldn't like it, I'm sure, if you didn't take care of his pets."

"Oh, I wouldn't, for the world, have anything happen to them, as he was so fond of them and kind to them," said the mother of the Curlytops. "But we could sell them to some animal store, and, as my husband says, give the money to a home for children. Uncle Toby would like that."

"Yes, he was very fond of children and animals," said the housekeeper, as she seemed about to leave. "It's a pity he never had any of his own—any children, I mean," she quickly added. "He did have enough animals. You'd better keep 'em, your children seem fond of 'em," she added.

"Oh, the Curlytops love animals," agreed Mr. Martin. "In fact I like them myself, especially Tip and Top, the dogs. I never saw any better trick animals."

Tip and Top had quieted down now, as had the other animals after Bob had come in to get the pigeons.

"You'd better keep all of Uncle Toby's pets," she concluded. "I'm going now. Just pull the door shut after you and it will lock. The water is turned off and the house is all cleaned out. There isn't any food to spoil, except what the animals need, and you can take that with you. Uncle Toby said I was to go as soon as you arrived to have charge of his collection, and, as you are here, I'm going. Uncle Toby has hired a man to look after the house so it will be all right. Go and get your pigeons, Bob," she added. "Good-bye, everybody," and away she went.

For a moment Mr. and Mrs. Martin looked at each other. Then Mr. Nip, the parrot, broke the silence by saying:

"I'm a crack-crack-cracker!"

"You're a fire-cracker—at least your feathers are red enough for that," laughed Mrs. Martin. "Well, we seem to have the pets whether we want them or not," she told her husband. "We can't go away and leave them here. We can't stay in this house, and try to sell them, if the water is turned off and there is nothing to eat. I guess we'll have to take the pets home with us, Dick."

Mr. Martin looked puzzled.

"Oh, yes! Please keep them!" begged Ted and Janet.

"An' det a han'-ordan fo' de monkey!" begged Trouble, speaking rather more in baby fashion than he usually talked, because he was so excited, I suppose.

"At least we'll have to take charge of Uncle Toby's pets until we decide what to do," said Mr. Martin, after a while. "We might keep some of them and sell the others."

"Oh, keep them *all*!" exclaimed Ted.

"We'll see," his father answered, and from the tone of his voice Ted and his sister were almost sure they would be allowed to have all the animals for their very own. Of course Trouble could hardly expect a hand-organ to go with Jack, the monkey, but that was not much of a loss.

"We can't get back home to-night," said Mrs. Martin, "that's sure. It's too far. We'll have to stay either here, at Uncle Toby's house, or at a hotel."

"I suppose we could stay here, if we had to," her husband remarked. "I can turn the water on, and it is easy enough to get something to eat, even if we have to buy it at the delicatessen shop."

"I just love delicatessen stuff, don't you?" whispered Jan to her brother. "I hope they get a lot! I'll give some to Snuff, the Persian cat."

"If we stay it will be just like camping," agreed Ted.

While Mr. and Mrs. Martin were considering what to do, Bob, the boy who had come for the pigeons, put his head in through the doorway and called out:

"I got 'em all, thank you! I'm going now. I hope you have good luck with Uncle Toby's pets!"

"Goodness knows we'll need it," said Mrs. Martin, and then she had to laugh. The whole affair seemed to her to be so very funny. Neither she nor her husband had imagined that Uncle Toby's "collection" could be anything like this—dogs, a parrot, a monkey, a Persian cat and a little alligator, not forgetting the white rats and mice.

"Well, we'd better stay here for the night," finally decided Daddy Martin. "It is warm, and Uncle Toby had quite a number of beds. The house is in good order. I'll turn on the water, and you and the children might go to the store and get things for supper," he added. "It will soon be night."

"Oh, what fun! We're going to stay here!" cried Janet, dancing around the Persian cat, who was trying to rub against her legs.

"And I'll teach Tip and Top some new tricks, so we can have a circus when we get home," remarked Ted.

"There's circus enough here," his father said, with a smile. "But trot along, Curlytops, if you are going to get something for us to eat. The animals have been fed and now it is time

Howard R. Garis

for us. I'm getting hungry."

"Me hundry, too!" declared Trouble.

"We mustn't let that happen!" laughed his mother. "We'll go to the store. Come along, Curlytops!"

As the children walked down the street with their mother to look for the nearest delicatessen store, they saw the boy Bob carefully wheeling his basket of pigeons toward his own home. He had gotten the birds out of Uncle Toby's barn.

When Mrs. Martin and the Curlytops, with Trouble, of course, came back to Uncle Toby's house, they found Daddy Martin sitting in front of the kitchen stove in which he had kindled a fire. In his lap was the Persian cat, purring contentedly, and Mr. Martin was rubbing the long, soft silky fur of Snuff.

In front of the father of the Curlytops were Skyrocket, Tip, and Top, the three dogs. They were lying asleep near the fire. In the other room were the mice, the rats, the alligator, the monkey, and the parrot, all the animals quiet, for a wonder, as Mrs. Martin said.

"Oh, Daddy! you love 'em, don't you?" exclaimed Jan, as she saw her father surrounded by some of the pets. "We may keep them, mayn't we?"

"I'll see about it," was the answer, and Janet whispered to Teddy that she was almost sure this meant "yes."

It did not take long to get up a little supper. Daddy Martin ran the automobile into the side yard of Uncle Toby's house, and the Curlytop family, as I sometimes call them, prepared to stay all night. There were plenty of beds, and in the morning they could turn off the water again, take the pets away, close the house, and everything would be as Uncle Toby wished it.

You can easily guess that neither of the Curlytops, nor Trouble, for that matter, wanted to go to bed early that night. The children were thinking too much of the pets. And, indeed, the pets seemed to like the children. Mr. Nip, the parrot, let Jan scratch his head, a form of caress of which he seemed very fond. Jack, the monkey, no longer snatched off Trouble's cap. But perhaps that was because baby William did not wear it near the lively chap. Snuff, the Persian cat, seemed to have taken a great liking to Mr. Martin, and as for the dogs, Tip and Top, they were hardly out of the sight of Jan and Ted. Nor was Skyrocket neglected or jealous. He entered into the fun of playing around on the lawn and porch with the white poodles after supper.

Even Slider, the little alligator, seemed very friendly. He took bits of meat from the fingers of Ted, though Janet said she was afraid of the scaly creature.

"I'm going to teach him some tricks, so he can be in the animal circus," declared Ted.

"Are you going to have a circus?" asked his sister.

"Sure!" he answered, though, to tell the truth, he had not begun to think of it until he saw all the pets Uncle Toby had left. "We'll have a fine circus!"

The evening passed pleasantly. Finally Trouble became sleepy, even though he was much interested in watching Jack, the monkey, crack peanuts.

"Come, laddie, you must go to bed!" called Mrs. Martin.

"Mr. Nip, the parrot, has gone to sleep long ago, with his head under his wing, poor thing!" and she sang part of the "Robin Song."

"Me want see head's under swing," murmured Trouble. "Me see!"

"Oh, no! I don't want to wake up Mr. Nip. He has a cloth over his cage to keep him quiet," and Mrs. Martin carried Trouble over to where the parrot's cage had been covered with a table-cover for the night.

"Goo'-bye," murmured the little fellow sleepily, and then he was carried up to his bed in Uncle Toby's house.

A little later Ted and Janet also went to their rooms, having given farewell pats and rubs to the dogs and cat. Mr. Martin went about, seeing that the house was locked up, and then he and his wife sat downstairs, talking while the children were asleep.

"Do you really intend to take all those pets home with us?" asked Mrs. Martin.

"I don't see what else we can do," her husband replied. "The children will be disappointed if we don't. And I don't really want to sell them. Uncle Toby might not like it. I think I'll take them home with us, and write to him, if I can get his address. He must have left it, even if he is going to live in South America."

"But how can we take home a monkey, a parrot, three dogs, a cat, an alligator and some rats and some white mice?" asked the mother of the Curlytops.

"Oh, there is plenty of room in the auto," her husband

answered. "We'll load it up in the morning."

The night passed quietly enough, except that about twelve o'clock the parrot suddenly began shrieking:

"Police! Police! Burglars! Police! I'm a crack-crack-cracker!"

"Dick! Dick! Wake up!" called Mrs. Martin. "Someone is at the front door!"

"Police! Police!" chattered the parrot again.

And, surely enough, it was the police, though how the red and green bird knew it is more than I can say. A passing policeman, seeing the light in Uncle Toby's house, and having been told by Mrs. Watson, the housekeeper, on her way to her sister's, that the place was to be closed, had stopped to inquire.

"I thought it was burglars," said the policeman, after Daddy Martin had gone down to the front door and explained.

"That's what Mr. Nip did, too, I guess," said Mr. Martin.

"Who's Mr. Nip?" asked the officer.

"The parrot," said the father of the Curlytops. "He awakened us by his shrieking."

After the policeman had gone, the house became quiet again, and nothing more happened until morning. After breakfast the water was turned off, and the home of Uncle Toby was made ready for closing up until the old gentleman should return.

The parrot's cage, the box for the monkey, the little tank of water and pebbles in which Slider lived, and the wire cage of the white mice and rats—all these were taken out to the automobile. It was a large one, and there was plenty of room for the Curlytops and their new pets.

"Take Snuff, the cat, in between you and Trouble, Janet," her father advised. "Tip and Top can snuggle down with Skyrocket on the floor near Ted. Are we all ready now?"

"As ready as we ever shall be," his wife answered. "My, what a queer load!" she said, with a laugh, as she looked back at the collection and the children. "People will think we're a traveling menagerie!"

This, however, did not worry the Curlytops. They liked it, and, a little later, they were on their way back toward Cresco. The Curlytops liked their new pets, and they also loved those they had had for a longer time—Skyrocket and Turnover.

"We'll try to get home early," said Mr. Martin to his wife, as he steered the automobile through the streets of Pocono. "We'll have to fix up a place for these pets."

"Yes," agreed his wife. "They are going to be quite a care. But the children will love them."

They stopped for lunch at a little restaurant, and the children were afraid lest some of their pets might escape while the meal was being served. But Mr. Martin saw a young man, sitting in front of a barber shop next to the restaurant, and said to him:

"Will you watch may automobile and the animals while we are in the dining room? I'll give you fifty cents."

"I'll be glad to do it," said the young man.

So long as he was on guard the Curlytops were satisfied. But when they came out they made a sad discovery. Ted jumped up on the running-board and looked down into the automobile to make sure all the pets were safe. The alligator, the parrot, the white mice and rats, the cat, the monkey, and two dogs were there. But there was no sign of Tip, the white poodle with a black spot on the end of his tail.

"Where is Tip? Oh, where is Tip?" cried Ted. "He's gone!"

CHAPTER VII

A FUZZY BURGLAR

"What's that?" asked Mr. Martin, who was the last of the Curlytop family to come out of the restaurant. "Who is gone? One of the pets?"

"Tip is gone," answered Teddy. "Oh, where is he?"

"Maybe he's hiding back of the monkey's cage," suggested Janet, for Jack, the pet monkey, lived in a sort of cage, or box, and he had been moved from Uncle Toby's house in it.

"No, Tip isn't here at all," said Teddy. "Top is here and Skyrocket, but Tip is gone."

"That can't be," said the young man who had said he would guard the animals while the Curlytops ate. "I've been here all the while, and I didn't see even one of the white mice get away."

He seemed to be a nice, good-natured young man, and appeared to be as much surprised as Teddy and Janet were over the loss of Tip. As for Trouble, he was not worrying much. He had climbed into the front seat of the automobile, and was playing with Snuff, the yellow Persian cat. As long as Trouble had some animal near him he did not worry much about anything else.

"Have you been right here all the while, young man?" asked Mr. Martin of the youth who had been left on guard. "You didn't go away, did you, and give someone a chance to come up and take one of the dogs?"

"Oh, no, sir! I stayed right here all the while. I sat down on the running-board and waited. The only thing that happened was that the alligator tried to crawl out, but I put him back. I was sitting here, thinking how funny it was that anybody should have so many pets, when, all of a sudden, I felt something rough on my neck."

"What was it?" asked Janet, while Teddy was looking under the automobile, thinking that perhaps Tip might be hiding there.

"It was the little alligator, with his rough tail," explained the young man, who said he was called "Shorty" by his chums. He was very tall, and perhaps that was why he was called "Shorty," in fun you know. "It was the little alligator that was crawling up my shoulder and scratching my neck," he explained. "I put him back in his cage, or tank, or whatever you call it, though I was afraid he'd bite me."

"Oh, no, Slider is very gentle," said Ted, who came up on the sidewalk, after having peered under the automobile. "Oh, dear, I don't see where Tip can be!" he said.

"It is queer that he should go away and leave Top," said Mrs. Martin, for the other white poodle dog was there, safe in the automobile.

Top looked up at the friends gazing down at him, barked and

wagged his tail. Perhaps he, too, was asking what had become of his chum, Tip.

"The dog must have jumped out on the opposite side of the car from where you were sitting," said Mr. Martin to Shorty. "Though if that had happened I should have thought you would have heard him," and the father of the Curlytops looked rather sharply at Shorty.

"No, sir, I didn't hear a thing," was the answer. "All I know is that the alligator tried to crawl up my neck. I didn't see the dog run away."

"Perhaps he didn't run away," suggested Mrs. Martin.

"What do you mean?" asked Janet.

"I mean someone may have stepped up softly, when this young man had his back turned, and, reaching over, may have lifted Tip up and taken him away. I wish you had sat in the auto, Shorty, instead of outside on the step."

"Yes'm, I wish so myself," agreed the young man. "But there were so many animals in there I thought I'd better be on the outside so I could chase 'em quicker in case any got away. And one did get away and I never saw him! I'm terribly sorry! I'll go down the street and see if I can find him."

"I wish you would," remarked Mr. Martin. "Just take a look, and ask everyone you meet if he saw a white poodle with a black tip on the end of his tail. If you find him I'll give you a dollar besides the fifty cents for watching the auto."

"I'd like to earn that dollar!" said the young man. "I'll go look!"

"I'll come, too," offered Teddy, "but I don't want a dollar if I find Tip. I just want to get our dog back."

"So do I," added Janet. "I'll come and look with you."

"This was a valuable dog," explained Mr. Martin, as Shorty moved off down the street. "He could do tricks. I'd like very much to get him back."

"I'll do my best," promised the young man. "It was my fault, in a way, that he got a chance to go away. I should have been looking on both sides of the auto at once, but I didn't. I'll see if I can't find him."

"I think I'll take a look, myself," said Mr. Martin to his wife, who had now gotten in the automobile with Trouble. "I don't like the way things have happened."

"Why, do you think that young man had anything to do with Tip's going away?" asked Mrs. Martin, as Ted and Janet went down the street one way while Shorty took the other direction.

"I can't be sure," answered the father of the Curlytops. "He looks like an honest young man, but if he knew what a valuable dog Tip was he might have let some friend of his step up and take away the pet animal."

"But wouldn't he have allowed both of the dogs to be taken—Top as well as Tip?" asked Mrs. Martin.

"Maybe there wasn't time to take but the one," her husband explained. "And perhaps I am wrong, and Shorty is right. Tip may have seen some other dog on the far side of the street, and have jumped out of the car to go up to him. It's too bad, but maybe we'll get him back."

Howard R. Garis

"I hope the children don't go so far away that they are lost, too," remarked Mrs. Martin.

"I think they'll not go far," said her husband. "Oh, no, you don't!" he suddenly exclaimed. "Come back here! We don't want to chase *you*!" and he made a hasty grab for Slider, the pet alligator, who seemed to want to get out of his glass-sided tank. "I'll be glad when we get Uncle Toby's menagerie safely home," said Mr. Martin.

"So shall I," his wife added. "Though the animals seem very nice. Trouble loves Snuff already."

"Oh, I suppose we shall get to like them all," agreed Mr. Martin. "We'll have to let Ted and Janet make places for them in the barn. It is warm weather now, and even the tropical animals, like the monkey, can stay out there."

"I wonder if the parrot will talk much?" ventured Mrs. Martin. "I have always rather wished for a talking parrot. Hello, Polly!" she called to the red and green bird in his cage.

"Hello, Polly!" answered Mr. Nip. "I'm a crack-crack-cracker!" he shouted at the top of his voice, and several persons, passing along the street, turned to smile at the Martins with their automobile load of pets. Then Mr. Nip began to whistle, so very much like a boy, that Skyrocket, Ted's dog, imagined his master was whistling to him, and barked in answer. Then Top, the remaining pet poodle, also began to bark, and Jack, the monkey, chattered in his own queer way.

"I'm a crack-crack-cracker!" Mr. Nip shouted at the top of his voice, and by this time quite a little crowd had gathered around the automobile.

"I wish we were at home!" exclaimed Mrs. Martin, who did not like so many strange persons staring at her and her husband and Trouble. But Trouble, who was trying to smooth down the fluffy fur of the Persian cat, did not seem to mind.

"What's this—a traveling circus?" asked a policeman, stepping up to the side of the car. "You have to get a permit if you're going to give a parade," he added to Mr. Martin.

"Oh, I'm not going to give a parade," answered the father of the Curlytops. "We are just waiting to see if we can find one of our pets, a trick dog that ran away—or that was taken away," and he explained what had happened.

"Do you know anything about that young man—Shorty he called himself—who watched our auto while we ate?" asked Mrs. Martin.

"I know him—yes," the policeman answered. "Sometimes he is bad, again he is good. I'd say he was bad more often than he was good."

"Just what I was afraid of!" exclaimed Mr. Martin. "I think Shorty knows more about the missing dog than he has told us. I don't believe he'll come back to get the dollar I promised him."

"Here come Ted and Janet," said their mother. "They didn't find Tip, either."

The Curlytops were hurrying along the street toward the automobile. They saw the policeman and began to run.

"Oh, did you find him? Did you get Tip back?" gasped Janet, as she reached the car. "Did the policeman find him?"

"No," answered her mother. "Did you see anything of our new dog, Curlytops?"

Ted and Janet sadly shook their heads. They had looked up and down several streets, they explained, but Tip was nowhere in sight. Nor had they seen Shorty since he, also, started to look for the missing animal.

"Well, we can't stay here much longer," decided Mr. Martin. "If we do, some more of Uncle Toby's pets may run away. We'd better get home. I'll leave you my name and address," said the father of the Curlytops to the policeman. "And if you hear anything of the missing dog please let me know."

"I will," promised the officer. "And if I see Shorty I'll make him tell me what really happened. Sometimes he plays jokes, and this may have been one of those times."

Mr. Martin waited a little longer, and when the young man did not come back, and when there was no sign of the missing Tip, it was thought best to start for Cresco. So, with one of Uncle Toby's pets missing, the trip was resumed.

"You certainly have pets enough, even without Tip," said Mrs. Martin, as they neared the home of the Curlytops.

"Yes, but we want Tip," said Teddy. "We can't give a good show with only one trick dog, 'specially when they are supposed to work as a team—one on the other's back."

"Are you going to give a show?" asked his mother.

"Yes," Teddy answered. "We'll give a show and make money. We can ask real money to see all the animals we have," and he looked down at the parrot's cage, the box of Jack, the monkey, the cage of the white mice and rats, and the tank of the alligator.

"Perhaps you could train Skyrocket to take the place of Tip," said Mr. Martin.

"Maybe," agreed Teddy. "But Skyrocket isn't the same kind of a dog, and Tip and Top looked so cute together."

"Just like twins," added Janet. "Oh, I hope we get Tip back."

They could not be sure whether the pet dog had run away himself, or whether someone had reached in over the side of the car and lifted him out. Someone may have done that while Shorty turned his back, saying nothing and not trying to stop him.

"I am sorry, but I think Shorty had something to do with Tip getting away," said Mr. Martin. "If that young man had been honest he would have come back and told us he couldn't find the dog. I should not have allowed Shorty to watch our auto. But it is too late, now, to be sorry."

The Curlytops reached their home just before supper, and there was so much to do, making places in the barn for Uncle Toby's pets, seeing that they were comfortable, and that they could not get out during the night, that, for a time, Ted and Janet forgot about the loss of Tip. If he had been the only pet, of course they would have missed him very much. But they had so many now that they were kept busy. Still, they wished, very much, that Tip could be found.

"For if we don't find him, we can't have half so many tricks in our circus show," said Teddy.

In due time the pets were put away for the night. The barn was a good place for them, and after they had been fed and given fresh water, which all pets need as much as they do food, the children left the animals to themselves.

"In the morning we'll start getting ready for the circus," declared Ted.

"Will dey be han'-ordan music?" asked Trouble.

"Well, we'll have some kind of music, if I have to toot on some tissue paper over a comb," answered Teddy.

Tired out with their two days' automobile trip, the Curlytops were soon ready for bed. Trouble went to sleep earlier than did Ted or Janet, but soon they, too, were ready to go to their rooms.

"Let us feed the animals—don't you do it, please," Ted begged of his father and mother. "Janet and I want to make believe we are keepers in a circus, feeding lions and tigers."

"All right, you may feed them," agreed their mother.

How long they had been asleep neither Ted nor Janet knew, but they were suddenly awakened in the night by hearing screams. The screams came from the open window of the house next door, where Mrs. Blake, a very nice lady, lived with her two servants. Her husband was dead, and her children had married and gone away. Mrs. Blake's bedroom was opposite the adjoining sleeping rooms of Ted and Janet, and often the Curlytops would call "good morning" across to Mrs. Blake.

But this time it was Mrs. Blake who called, and she did not exactly call, she screamed in the middle of the night.

"Help! Help!" cried the lady from her open window. "Mr.

Martin! Mary Ann! Patrick!" (these were her servants) "come and get him. A little fuzzy burglar is in my room! Come and get the fuzzy burglar!"

Howard R. Garis

CHAPTER VIII

SLIDER GOES SLIDING

Teddy and Janet, sleeping in their rooms on the side of their house nearest to the home of Mrs. Blake, were the first to be awakened by the screams of the frightened lady. For that Mrs. Blake was frightened anyone could tell who heard her cry.

"Come and take the fuzzy burglar! Take the fuzzy burglar out of my room!" she exclaimed again and again.

By this time Teddy had jumped out of his bed and had run to his window. At the same time Janet, in the next room, had jumped out of her bed and had run to her window. Both children looked across the yard to the home of Mrs. Blake. They could see her, in the moonlight, standing at her window.

"What's the matter, Curlytops?" called their mother, across the hall. She had been awakened, not so much by the cries of Mrs. Blake as by the movements of Ted and Janet. "What's the matter?" asked Mrs. Martin.

"There's a funny burglar over in Mrs. Blake's house, and she wants someone to come and get it," answered Janet.

"No, she didn't say *funny* burglar—she said *fuzzy*!" declared Ted.

"Well, anyhow, it's a *burglar*," declared Janet.

And from the other house again came the appeal:

"Patrick! Mary Ann! Mr. Martin! Somebody! Come and get the fuzzy burglar!"

By this time Mr. Martin, who had gotten up, had been told by his wife that something was wrong in Mrs. Blake's house. He put on some clothes and hurried downstairs, carrying a flashlight in one hand and his revolver in the other.

"Oh!" exclaimed Janet, who, with Teddy, watched her father go, "Daddy's going to shoot the funny burglar."

"*Fuzzy* burglar!" corrected Ted.

But Janet had covered her ears with her hands, so she would not hear her father shoot his revolver—in case he found anything to shoot at—so the little girl did not hear what her brother said.

Mr. Martin ran across the lawn to the front porch of Mrs. Blake's house. By this time several other neighbors had been awakened be the lady's screams, and some of the men came out, partly dressed, to see what was going on.

"Come in, Mr. Martin," said Patrick, as he opened the door for the father of the Curlytops. Patrick was Mrs. Blake's gardener.

"What is it, Patrick?" asked Mr. Martin, holding his revolver in one hand and the flashlight in the other. "Where is the burglar?"

"I didn't see anything, Mr. Martin," answered the gardener. "I heard Mrs. Blake scream, and I got up, and so did Mary Ann, the cook, but we can't find anything!"

"But there *is* a burglar here!" said Mrs. Blake from the head of the stairs, where she now stood. "I was awakened by a noise in my room, and when I looked at the window, I saw in the moonlight, sitting on the sill, a fuzzy little old man. He's a burglar, I'm sure of it, and I wish the police would come!"

"I think there are enough of us here now, Mrs. Blake, to look after two or three burglars without the police," said Mr. Martin, as he glanced at several neighbors who had come in. "Let's have a look around," he went on. "I fancy, if there was a burglar, that he has gotten away by this time."

"I hope he has gotten away, and will never come back," said Mrs. Blake. "But I wish you gentlemen would look, just the same."

So Mr. Martin and the other men neighbors, with Patrick, the gardener, to help, began a search of the house. They went to Mrs. Blake's room first.

"I don't see any burglar," said Mr. Martin. He did not need his electric flashlight now, as the house had been lighted from top to bottom by Mrs. Blake's two servants.

"There he is! There he is!" suddenly cried Mrs. Blake. "Under that big chair. There's the fuzzy burglar!"

Mr. Martin and two or three other men rushed over to the chair at which Mrs. Blake pointed. Mr. Martin stooped down, and then he laughed.

"What's the matter?" asked Mr. Tyndall, a neighbor from across the street.

"I'll show you," answered Mr. Martin, as he thrust his arm under the chair. "Come out of there, Jack!" he went on, and out from beneath the chair he pulled—Jack, Uncle Toby's pet monkey! Poor Jack was as much frightened as Mrs. Blake had been, but he cowered down in Mr. Martin's arms and looked up into the face of the father of the Curlytops as if saying:

"Please don't whip me! I didn't mean to be bad!"

The men who had come in to help hunt a burglar looked at the fuzzy monkey in Mr. Martin's arms, and then burst out laughing.

"Yes, it must have been him that I saw perched on my window," said Mrs. Blake. "In my alarm, it did look like a fuzzy, little old man, and of course I thought it was a burglar. I was foolish. It was a very small burglar. I didn't know you kept monkeys, Mr. Martin."

"I only keep one," he said, "and I don't exactly keep that, myself. It's one of the children's pets. It used to belong to my Uncle Toby, and we just brought Jack home this afternoon. We put him in the barn with the white mice and the alligator—"

"Don't tell me there's an *alligator* running around loose!" cried Mrs. Blake. "Oh, a monkey is bad enough, but an *alligator*—"

"It's only a little one," said Mr. Martin. "And I'm sorry Jack got loose and frightened you. I'll see, after this, that the pets don't get out at night."

"Oh, I'm sure I don't want to spoil the children's pleasure in the least," went on Mrs. Blake. "But I didn't know you had such a menagerie next door to me, Mr. Martin."

"We didn't have until to-day—or rather, yesterday, for it is now past midnight," Mr. Martin explained. "My Uncle Toby left me his collection of animals when he went away suddenly, and Ted and Janet say they are going to have a circus."

"Save me a ticket!" cried Mr. Hanson, who lived two or three houses down the street.

"And I want one," added Mr. Fenton. "If the Curlytops give a circus I want to come to it!"

"So do it!" cried several other neighbors, who had turned out to see what all the excitement was about.

"I'll tell Teddy and Janet," promised Mr. Martin, as he carried Jack out of Mrs. Blake's house, much to the relief of that lady, though she was rather fond of animals in general.

So the excitement quieted down, and after it was all over a policeman came along, one of the neighbors having telephoned in the first alarm. But there was nothing for the officer to do.

"Now, Curlytops," said Mr. Martin, at breakfast the next morning when the excitement of the night was being talked over, "if you are to keep Uncle Toby's pets here, we must be careful that they do not bother the neighbors. Your own dog and cat are very good, and make no trouble. But with a monkey, a parrot, another dog and cat, to say nothing of the alligator and the white mice, we may cause a lot of trouble to our good neighbors. And we wouldn't want to do that."

"What do you want us to do, Daddy?" asked Ted. He had just fed the two dogs—Skyrocket and Top, while Janet had poured out some milk for Turnover and Snuff, the two cats.

"We must make cages that can be locked at night, or else we must make sure that the barn is tightly closed," said his father. "I don't suppose, during the day, that there will be much trouble. It is at night we must be careful. No one likes to be awakened by seeing a monkey on the window sill."

"I wouldn't care," said Teddy.

"Well, ladies like Mrs. Blake don't care for such thrills," returned Mr. Martin, with a laugh. "So we must be sure that all the members of our menagerie are safely caged each night. I shall depend on you Curlytops for that."

"We'll be careful!" promised Teddy.

"I'll help you lock up every night," added Janet.

"Well, then I will leave the pets to you Curlytops," said their father. "It is on your account that your mother and I are keeping them instead of selling them, and while they will be some care, we do not mind if you do your share."

"The first thing I'm going to do," said Teddy, when he and Janet were left to themselves, their father going to his store, "is to see how many tricks Top can do."

"Isn't it too bad we haven't Tip?" said Janet. "They were so cute together!"

"Yes," agreed her brother. "But maybe I can make Skyrocket let Top ride on his back, and teach 'em some other tricks. Come here, Top!" he called to the white poodle with the black spot on top of his head. "Let's see you walk on your hind legs."

Top was very willing to do this, and while Ted and Janet sat on boxes in the barn, with their other pets around them, Uncle Toby's poodle went through his performance. When he had walked on his hind legs in a little circle he suddenly sneezed.

"Oh, maybe he's catching cold!" cried Janet.

"No, I think that was a trick," suggested Teddy. "Sneeze, Top!" he ordered. Surely enough, the poodle sneezed, and he would do it every time Teddy or Janet told him to.

"Oh, he knows two tricks, besides the one he does with Tip," Teddy said in delight. "Maybe he does a lot more. I wish Uncle Toby had written them down, so we'd know what the dogs can do for our circus."

"We can write to Uncle Toby, when daddy gets the address, and ask about the tricks," Janet said.

"Yes," agreed Teddy, "we can do that. I wonder if Slider can do any tricks?" he asked, when Top had been rewarded for his efforts with a little bone to gnaw.

"Do alligators do tricks?" asked Janet, as she reached in through the bars of Mr. Nip's cage and scratched the head of the red and green parrot.

"I guess they do," Teddy answered. "If they don't we'll teach our Slider to do a trick. I'm going to take him out of his tank."

The cage of the little pet alligator was a sort of tank, in the bottom of which was some water, and in this were little pebbles, like those in some goldfish bowls. The tank stood near a window in the barn where the sun shone in, for Mr. Martin had told the Curlytops that their pets who lived in warm, or tropical, countries must be kept where it was warm and sunny. That was what they were used to in their native lands.

So Slider had a warm, sunny place, and now Teddy took the scaly creature out of the tank and put him on a box, where the sun could shine on the long-tailed fellow.

As it happened, there was a long, smooth board resting on the upper edge of this box and extending down to the barn floor. Teddy had laid the board slanting fashion on the box when he was making room for the cage of Jack, the monkey.

For a little while, after he had been placed in the warm sun on top of the box, the alligator remained quiet, slowly blinking his eyes. Then he began to crawl.

"That isn't much of a trick," declared Janet.

"Oh, I haven't started to teach him a trick yet," her brother answered. "I'm trying to think what an alligator can do best."

But Slider, as he was called, because he seemed to slide around in such a slow, easy fashion, took matters into his own claws, so to speak.

He crawled around on his box top and then managed to clamber up on the slanting board, one edge of which rested on the box.

"I wonder if he is going to slide down-hill," said Janet in a low voice, as if she did not want to disturb the little alligator.

Howard R. Garis

And then, just as if he had made up his mind to do that very thing, Slider wiggled along until he was only holding to the edge of the slanting board by his two hind feet, while his long tail was only partly on the box. A moment later, giving himself a hitch like a boy getting his sled over the top of the hill, Slider went sliding down the smooth, slanting board.

Down he slid until he reached the barn floor, and as there was some smooth straw at the point where the board rested, Slider slid across this straw for several feet.

"Oh, did you see that?" cried Janet.

"See it? I should say I did!" cried Teddy. "Slider slid all right! That's going to be his trick! I'll make a longer board slide, and I'll put the lower end in a pan of water, so when Slider slides down he'll make a splash! That will be a fine trick for the circus! Come on, Slider, slide again!"

Teddy was just lifting up his pet alligator, intending to put him on the top of the slanting board, when Trouble was heard calling:

"Oh, come an' 'ook at Snuff! Come an' 'ook at Snuff! He's doin' suffin' funny!"

CHAPTER IX

MRS. JOHNSON'S BABY

Teddy and Janet turned their attention from Slider, the pet alligator whose new trick they had just discovered, to Trouble, their little brother.

"What's that you say?" asked Teddy, putting the alligator back again on the box on which stood the tank of water.

"You ought to see Snuff," repeated the little fellow.

"What's he doing?" asked Janet.

"Oh, he's rollin' ober an' ober in yard," explained Trouble, so excited that he did not take time to talk as straight as usual. "He's rollin' funny!"

"Oh, maybe the poor cat has a fit!" exclaimed Janet. "That would be too bad, Ted! He couldn't be in our circus."

"I'll go see," offered Teddy. He had been among animals so long, and was so kind to them, and he liked them so much, that he was not afraid to try to help even a sick one. And a cat that has a fit is ill, and needs medicine. Sometimes Turnover became ill, and had to be doctored, and more than

Howard R. Garis

once Skyrocket, the dog, was in need of some simple home remedy.

So the first thought of Janet and Ted, when Trouble told them that Snuff, the cat they had brought from Uncle Toby's, was "rollin'"—their first thought, I say, was that Snuff had a fit.

"You stay here and watch Slider," said Ted to his sister, "and I'll go out into the yard and see what's the matter with the cat."

"I go, too," added Trouble. "I 'ike to see Snuff roll!"

"No, you had better stay here with me," suggested Janet, and she ran to the barn door to catch hold of her little brother before he could toddle after Teddy.

"I want to go! Lemme go!" cried Trouble, and he struggled to get away from Janet.

"No, you must stay with sister," said the little girl, as pleasantly as she could. "Look, I'll show you a new trick that Slider, our pet alligator, can do. Trouble like to see Slider do a trick?" she asked. "Come on, Trouble! See Slider do his sliding trick!"

Baby William was not proof against this attraction. He ceased trying to pull away from Janet and let her lead him back to the alligator's tank. There Janet took up the scaly, long-tailed creature, which was idly crawling around, and put him on top of the slanting board, as Teddy had been about to do when Trouble told about Snuff. Janet did not mind picking up Slider.

The Curlytops were not afraid of animals that many girls and boys do not like to handle. Janet and Teddy knew a great deal about snakes, and they knew that only two kinds that lived in their State were harmful. These were the rattlesnake and the copperhead. All other kinds, such as black snakes, milk snakes and garter snakes can never harm a person. Teddy and Janet knew this, and they had been taught by their father that these harmless snakes did a great deal of good by eating rats and mice that, otherwise, would spoil the farmers' grain.

So it was that Janet had learned to pick up even large black snakes, knowing they would not harm her, and once she and her brother had even tamed a good-sized black snake, so that it would let the children pick it up, and it would lie, coiled, in their lap.

Snakes can not be tamed, or made to do tricks like other animals, and the stories of "snake charmers" are mostly untrue. Some snakes may rise and sway when music is played, and the snakes that circus performers handle are just as harmless as the garden snakes you see. Some of the larger ones, however, are very powerful, and can twist themselves around a person or an animal strongly enough to kill. But the performers know how to handle snakes, using slow and gentle movements, so the reptiles do not mind it.

Thus it was that Janet had no fear of Slider, the pet alligator. She lifted him up, put him on top of the slanting board and, just as he had done before, Slider went sliding down.

"Oh! Oh!" cried Trouble in delight.

"Isn't that a good trick?" asked Janet, laughing with her little brother. "Aren't you glad you stayed with me."

"Yes, I is glad," declared Trouble. "Now Trouble make

Slider slide."

"All right," agreed Janet.

Baby William was not much more afraid of animals, snakes included, than were Teddy and Janet. So his sister let him pick up Slider and give the alligator another coast down the board hill.

I am not saying that Slider would have done this trick himself, even after much practice. It was mostly an accident, I believe, his coasting down the board when he got to the slanting edge. The alligator just naturally crawled around and, reaching the edge, he fell over, and coasted down. Janet and Trouble put him close to the edge on purpose, so he would go down, knowing that it did not hurt the alligator in the least. I suppose a mud turtle would have done the same "trick."

Reptiles have a very small brain, and can not be taught to do tricks as can dogs, horses and cats, and the alligator, the turtle and the snake belong to the class known as reptiles. So though the children called what Slider did a "trick," it was more like an accident, though it was not a harmful one.

"Me make Slider slide," exclaimed Trouble, and, surely enough, when he had put Uncle Toby's scaly pet on the board, down the alligator slid.

Trouble and Janet were enjoying themselves in this fashion, and Janet was wondering what Teddy was doing, when that young member of the Curlytop family stuck his head in through the open barn door and called:

"Come on out and see Snuff!"

"Oh, has he a bad fit?" asked Janet.

"He hasn't got a fit at all!" answered Ted. "He's doing one of the best tricks you ever saw, and it will be dandy in our circus! Come and look at him!"

"Oh, I'm glad he hasn't a fit!" cried Janet. "Come on, Trouble!"

But now there was more trouble with Trouble, for he wanted to stay and play with Slider.

"Me see Slider slide more!" demanded the little fellow. And it was as hard for Janet to get him to come out of the barn now, as it had been to make him stay in before.

"Oh, come on and see Snuff do his funny trick!" she begged, and finally Trouble came away from the alligator.

"And it sure is a funny trick!" laughed Ted, who had waited for his little brother and Janet to come out. "Just you see!"

When the two Curlytops and Trouble hurried around the corner of the barn, Teddy pointed to Snuff, the new, big cat that had been brought from Uncle Toby's house.

Snuff was on top of a large leather ball, and it was rolling around the yard, with him on top of it, just as a clown in the circus stands upright on a large, painted ball, and rolls himself around the ring. This ball was a football that Teddy had owned for some time. The outside was leather, and inside was a rubber bladder that could be blown up. It was a round ball, of the kind used in "Association" games, and not for "Rugby," which most of the football elevens play in this country. The "Rugby" ball is shaped like a watermelon, but the other is more like a muskmelon, and it was on this latter kind of a ball that Snuff was rolling around the yard, just like a circus clown.

"Was this what Trouble meant when he said Snuff was rolling?" asked Janet.

"Yes," answered Teddy. "I'm glad Uncle Toby's cat didn't have a fit. Now we can make him do this trick in our animal circus."

"Oh, it's a lovely trick," declared Janet. "I wonder how he learned it?"

"Maybe Uncle Toby or the lady who owned him first taught Snuff to roll on top of a football," Ted answered, while the yellowish brown cat kept on stepping lightly this way and that, making the ball turn over and over. "I guess Trouble left the ball out here in the yard. He was playing with it last. Then Snuff must have come out, and when he saw the ball he remembered that he knew how to do a trick on it. And he got up and did it without anyone telling him."

"Maybe he won't do it any more," suggested Janet.

"We can soon see," Teddy said. "Here, Snuff!" he called to the big, friendly cat. "Come over here," and Teddy whistled as he did for Turnover. Snuff came as he was called, almost as a dog might do, and Turnover, also hearing the whistle by which Teddy summoned him to meals, came running around the corner of the barn.

"No, we haven't anything for you to eat now, pussies," said Ted, with a laugh. "But I'll give you something in a little while if Snuff does the football trick again."

After petting the two cats, and scratching them under their

ears, which they seemed to like very much. Teddy held Snuff in his arms, and told Janet to take up the football.

"We'll put it down in front of Snuff and see if he gets up on it," suggested Teddy. And when this was done the big cat from Uncle Toby's jumped out of Ted's arms, and leaped on top of the football, rolling it over and over just like a clown in a circus.

"Oh, it is a trick—a real trick!" cried Janet. "Wouldn't it be great if we could dress Snuff up in a little suit like a clown?"

"Maybe we can," said Teddy. "But it will be hard, as cats don't like to have fixin's on 'em as much as dogs do. I wonder who taught Snuff that trick? I guess it must have been Uncle Toby."

And, some time afterward, the Curlytops learned that it was their father's queer, animal-loving uncle who had taught Snuff to roll around on a football.

"I'm terrible glad Uncle Toby left us his collection, aren't you?" asked Janet of her brother, when Snuff had grown tired of doing his trick, and both cats were being fed.

"Yes," agreed Teddy, "I am. First I thought it might be a collection of stamps or coins. But I'm glad it was pets."

The Curlytops were going to have a great deal of fun with their pets, they were sure of that.

"If we only had Tip back," sighed Janet, as she and Teddy sat watching the cats eat, talking, meanwhile, about the circus they were going to have with all their animals.

"Yes, it's too bad one of Uncle Toby's dogs is gone," agreed

Teddy. "Of course we can do some tricks with Top, but it would be better with the two of them."

"I wonder if he jumped out of the auto and ran away, if someone picked him up off the seat, or if that man Shorty knows where he is?"

"That's what I wonder, too," replied Teddy. "And I wonder if we shall ever get Tip back?"

But many strange things were to happen to the Curlytops and their pets before this came about.

Teddy and Janet were so busy talking about the circus they were to get up with their animals that, for a time, they did not watch Trouble. That little chap wandered back to the barn, for he had been much interested in watching the alligator do his trick.

"Me make Slider slide some more," said Trouble, talking to himself, as he had a habit of doing. Into the barn he toddled. The alligator was swimming around in his small tank of water, but, being a tame and pet reptile, he came out when Trouble stood near the cage.

Unafraid of animals, as were Teddy and Janet, baby William picked Slider up and put him on the slanting board.

Down went the alligator as nicely as you please!

It was about half an hour after this that Teddy and Janet decided they would try to teach their dog Skyrocket some tricks to do with Top.

"Let's bring 'em both out here in the yard together," suggested Ted. "You get Skyrocket, Jan, and I'll hunt Top."

"All right," agreed his sister.

But before they had gone far, looking for the two dogs, they heard a cry of alarm from Mrs. Johnson, one of the neighbors across the street.

"Oh, my baby! My baby!" cried Mrs. Johnson, as she ran down off the porch toward a mosquito-netting covered carriage in the front yard. "A big snake is going to sting my baby! Oh, Trouble! what shall I do?"

"Ha! is Trouble over there?" asked Ted of Janet.

"Yes, and something else, too, I guess," was the answer.

And Mrs. Johnson called again:

"Oh, a big snake is in the carriage with my baby!"

CHAPTER X

MR. CAPPER'S BUNS

Forgetting in the excitement, all about teaching Skyrocket and Top to do some tricks together, as Tip and Top did before Tip was lost, Teddy and Janet ran across the street toward Mrs. Johnson, who was standing beside the carriage in which was her baby. Near her was Trouble, but the little fellow did not seem to be as excited as was Mrs. Johnson.

"Trouble," cried Janet, as she took hold of her little brother's arm, "did you tease Ruth?" Ruth was the name of Mrs. Johnson's baby, and though Trouble was, usually, a good little chap, he might have done something to make a baby cry, Janet realized.

"I didn't do nuffin'!" declared Trouble.

"Oh, no, Trouble is all right!" said Mrs. Johnson. "It's a big, black snake that has crawled into my baby's carriage. I put Ruth out here to have her sleep, and I looked from the window every once in a while to see that she was all right."

"And she was, for quite a while. But a moment ago, when I looked, I saw Trouble near the carriage, and then I saw a big, ugly snake crawling over Ruth's robe. Oh, where is it?

Where's the snake, darling? Did the snake bite you?" and Mrs. Johnson caught Ruth up from the carriage in her arms.

"I never knew a snake would crawl up into a baby carriage," said Teddy. "I don't see any; do you, Jan?"

"No," answered his sister, "I don't!"

"There it is! Look!" cried Mrs. Johnson, pointing with one hand, while she held Ruth close to her in her other arm. The baby had been rather rudely awakened from her sleep, and she was just getting ready to cry. Her lips were puckering up, and in another moment she would let out a yell. Janet and Teddy knew this, for they had, often enough, watched Trouble do the same thing when he was smaller.

"There's the snake!" exclaimed Mrs. Johnson, and, as she spoke and pointed, the Curlytops saw something black crawl out from among the folds of the robes in the baby carriage.

Ted had one glimpse of the head of the reptile, and then the boy cried:

"That isn't a snake! It's Slider, our pet alligator! How did he get here?"

"A pet alligator?" cried Mrs. Johnson. "In my Ruth's carriage! How did it get here?"

"I bringed it!" said Trouble, in the silence that followed.

"You what?" cried Janet.

"I bringed Slider ober to play wif Ruff!" said Trouble. "I play wif Slider in barn, and den hims hoots get tired, so I bringed him over to ride in de carriage wif Ruff."

"What does he mean?" asked Mrs. Johnson, crooning to "Ruff," as Trouble called the baby, and making the little one quiet. For William was using some of his "baby talk," which he often did when he was excited.

"He means that the alligator's feet got tired, I suppose," translated Janet. "He says 'hoots' for 'feet.' He must mean that Slider got tired of sliding down the board."

Mrs. Johnson looked from one Curlytop to the other, and then at Trouble. A puzzled look was on her face.

"Really, children dear," she said, "*you* may know what you are talking about, but *I* don't. What with hoots, Slider and a board I'm all mixed up!"

"I bringed him—I bringed Slider," explained Trouble.

"Yes, we know you did that," said Teddy. "But you shouldn't have, Trouble. It was wrong to take our pet out of the barn, and it was wrong to put Slider in the baby carriage."

"Yes, we didn't know Trouble was going to do anything like this," said Janet, apologizing for her little brother's misdeed. "But Ted and I were talking about what tricks we'd get Skyrocket and Top to do, now that Tip is gone. And we'd just got through watching Snuff do a new trick on top of a football, so we didn't watch Trouble very much."

"How many pets you have!" exclaimed Mrs. Johnson. "I suppose those are pets you have been talking about?" she asked.

"Ours and Uncle Toby's," answered Teddy. "We have more pets than we ever had before, and we're going to give a circus. Will you come, Mrs. Johnson?"

"An' bring Ruff!" invited Trouble.

There was a laugh at this.

"If you love Ruth you mustn't put Slider in her carriage any more," cautioned Janet, as she lifted the pet alligator out from among the blankets. "Little babies don't like alligators."

"All wite. I like 'em," said Trouble, and then he ran back across the street.

"We'll be going now," said Teddy to Mrs. Johnson. "We're sorry William made trouble."

"Oh, he didn't mean to," said Ruth's mother. "He's a dear little fellow. I must come over and see your pets. Ruth loves a pussy or a dog, but she doesn't know much about alligators."

"We have a monkey, too," said Janet.

"And a parrot named Mr. Nip," added her brother.

"And white rats and mice! They're real cute!" exclaimed Janet.

"I don't believe I would like the mice!" said Mrs. Johnson.

"But ours are white," Janet explained. "That makes a big difference. They're as nice as rabbits!"

"They wouldn't be for me," said Ruth's mother, with a laugh. "Good-bye, Curlytops! Come over again, and bring a pussy or doggie with you."

Ted and Janet promised they would, and then they hurried

back across the street after Trouble. They wanted to make sure he would not get into any more mischief with the pets.

Daddy Martin was told, that evening after supper, all that had happened during the day, from the discovery that Slider and Snuff could do tricks, to the finding of the pet alligator in baby Ruth's carriage.

"Well, it seems you had lots of excitement to-day," he said to his wife.

"Just a little," she agreed.

"But if Uncle Toby's pets are to make trouble I don't know that we can keep them," Daddy Martin said.

Teddy and Janet looked at each other.

"Oh, we can't let them go now!" exclaimed Teddy.

"We're just getting to love them!" his sister added.

"And we haven't found out any tricks yet that the white mice can do," Teddy went on. "We haven't even named 'em!"

"Well, I suppose if the neighbors don't complain I shouldn't," admitted Mr. Martin. "But with the monkey scaring Mrs. Blake, and the alligator scaring Mrs. Johnson—"

"They weren't very *much* scared," interrupted Ted. "Please let us keep Uncle Toby's pets! We want to give a circus."

"We'll see," said Mr. Martin. "I hope nothing more will happen, though, to annoy the neighbors."

"We'll watch our pets so they won't get out," promised Ted

and Janet.

The next few days were spent by the Curlytops in getting better acquainted with the animals that had been brought from Uncle Toby's. They liked their new pets more and more the more they saw of them. Of course they wished they could get Tip back, but that trick dog seemed to have vanished.

Daddy Martin put an advertisement in the paper, and offered a reward to whoever would bring Tip back, but there were no answers—at least none that amounted to anything. It is true that several men and boys came with strange dogs they thought answered the description of the missing Tip, but none of the animals was the pet so much wanted.

Nor was anything heard of the missing youth "Shorty." He seemed to have disappeared with the poodle, and the police said they believed Shorty knew where Tip was, and had, perhaps, taken him away in order to sell him.

"Well, of course we have enough animals without Tip to give a show," said Teddy. "But I'd love to get Tip back. And I guess Top is lonesome without him."

"I guess so, too," added Janet.

But if Top was lonesome he showed no signs of it after one or two days. He made friends with Skyrocket, as Snuff did with Turnover, and the dogs and cats lived happily together.

But alas for the hopes of Mr. Martin that his neighbors would not again be troubled by the pets of the Curlytops. It was about a week after the animals had been brought from Uncle Toby's house that, as Mr. Martin was coming home from the store rather early one afternoon, he saw a crowd in front of the bakeshop of Mr. Capper, just around the corner

Howard R. Garis

from the home of the Curlytops.

"I hope that isn't a fire in Mr. Capper's bakery," thought Daddy Martin, for more than once hot grease had boiled over in the bakeshop and caused slight fires.

As Mr. Martin approached Mr. Capper's store he heard loud laughter from the crowd of men and boys in front of the show window.

"It can't be a fire, or they wouldn't laugh," said the father of the Curlytops. "I wonder what it is?"

He hastened on, and as he came within view of the bakery window he uttered an exclamation of surprise. For there, among the buns, eating them and playing among the other cakes, were several large white rats and mice.

"Look at that one big one stand up on his hind legs and nibble a bun just like a squirrel!" said a man watching the antics of the white rats and mice among Mr. Capper's buns. If this man had only known it, squirrels and rats belong to the same family, that called "rodents," only a squirrel has a much larger tail than a rat or a mouse.

"I wonder what in the world Mr. Capper lets those white rats stay in his bakeshop window for?" thought Mr. Martin, as he ran up. "They are not harmful, of course, but people will not like to eat bakery stuff after rats and mice, even if they are white, have run around them. It's a poor advertisement."

At that moment the baker himself, who had been out in his oven-room, came running into the shop. He gave one look at his window, saw the white rats and mice playing around in and nibbling his choice buns, and then the baker cried:

"Oh, who did this? Who played this trick on me and spoiled my buns? Who let those mice in there?"

"Didn't you do it yourself?" asked Mr. Martin, who knew the baker very well, having traded with him for a number of years.

"Let those mice in my window? Never!" cried Mr. Capper. "Why should I do a thing like that?"

"I thought maybe it was for an advertisement—to attract customers to your store," said Mr. Martin. "Though I thought it was rather funny."

"It is too funny!" cried the baker. "All my buns are spoiled, and I just baked them. As for customers—I have a crowd, yes, but they will not buy what the mice have nibbled.

"Whose mice are they? Whose white rats are they? I ask you that!" cried the baker, who was much excited. "A little while ago two boys come in to buy cookies. I wait on them, and I go back to my oven. Then the next I know I see a crowd and I come out to find—these!"

He pointed to the white rats and mice that were having a fine time among the buns in the bakeshop window.

"You say two boys were here a little while ago?" asked Mr. Martin, and he began to have a suspicion of what had happened.

"Two boys," replied the baker. "They have a box with them—Ha! here is the box now. It is the cage that the mice got out of!" he cried, pointing to a box with a wire front on the floor of the store, in a corner.

"Uncle Toby's box!" exclaimed Mr. Martin, in a low voice.

"What's that?" cried the baker. "You know these white rats and mice, Mr. Martin?"

"I'm afraid I do," said the father of the Curlytops. "My children got some new pets from an uncle of mine—Uncle Toby. Among the pets were white mice and rats. That is the box we brought them in from Pocono. But how did the box get here?"

"Some boys brought it in, I am telling you," the baker answered. "Two boys."

"Did you know them? Was one my son Teddy?" asked Mr. Martin.

"I do not know—I forgot to look I was in such a hurry, for my bread was almost burning in my oven. I run to the store quick, as I am all alone now; I wait on the boys, they want cookies; and I run back to my oven. Now I come—the rats— the mice!" and Mr. Capper, who was a Frenchman, raised his hands in the air over his head in despair.

"I wonder if Ted could have done this?" mused Mr. Martin.

And then he heard Teddy's voice calling:

"Come on, Jim! Here they are! We left the rats here, and— Oh, I say! Look! They got out of the cage, and look what they're doing to the buns!"

A moment later Teddy Martin came pushing his way through the crowd now in the bakery.

CHAPTER XI

TOP ACTS STRANGELY

Mr. Martin, the father of the Curlytops, Mr. Capper, the baker, and the crowd of persons in the shop looked at Teddy and his friend, Jimmy Norton, as the two boys hurried into the place. Nearly everyone guessed what had happened, but Mr. Martin wanted to make sure, so he asked:

"Teddy, did you let your white mice and rats get loose among Mr. Capper's buns?"

"Well, I—I didn't exactly do it, Daddy," Teddy answered. "But I guess they did get loose, didn't they?" he asked, with half a smile.

"There is no doubt about it—they are loose, and they have done a lot of damage," and Mr. Martin spoke rather sternly.

"Damage! They have eaten up over two dollars' worth of buns—or they have as much spoiled!" said the excited baker.

"How did it happen?" asked Teddy's father.

"Well, it was an accident," the little Curlytop boy answered. "Jimmy and I were taking the cage down to the store to have some new wire put on. There's a place where the wire is broken, and it needed fixing so the rats couldn't get out. So Jimmy and I took the cage, and the rats and mice in it, down to the hardware store."

"Why didn't you take the mice out, and leave them in the barn?" asked Mr. Martin.

"'Cause there wasn't anything I could leave 'em in," Teddy replied. "I was afraid they'd get out, and maybe go over in Mrs. Johnson's baby carriage, just as Slider did. So I thought if we took the rats and mice right in the cage the man at the store could put some new wire netting over the old, and they couldn't get out."

"And did he do it?" Teddy's father went on, while the crowd listened to the talk.

"Yes, sir," Teddy replied. "The cage was fixed all right, and on the way back, Jimmy and I got tired of carrying it, so we stopped in here to get some cookies. We were hungry."

"It is as I told you!" broke in Mr. Capper. "Two boys did come in for cookies. These are the two—I remember now."

"Well, why didn't you boys take the cage of rats and mice with you when you went out?" asked Mr. Martin. "If you hadn't left them here they wouldn't have gotten loose and gone into Mr. Capper's show window to eat or spoil all his buns. Why did you leave the cage here?"

"We—we forgot it, I guess; didn't we, Jimmy?" asked Teddy of his chum.

"Yes," agreed Jimmy, "we did."

"But if the man at the hardware store put new wire on the cage, I don't see how the rats and mice got out," Mr. Martin went on.

Teddy looked at the empty cage which had been set down in a corner when he and his chum bought the cookies.

"The door came open!" Teddy exclaimed. "See, Daddy, the door sprang open and the white mice got out that way. It wasn't our fault at all!"

"But it was your fault for leaving the cage here," went on Mr. Martin. "I don't see why you did it."

"I guess it was on account of the fire engine," spoke up Jimmy Norton.

"The fire engine!" cried Teddy's father. "What has the fire engine to do with white mice eating buns?"

"Well, after we'd bought the cookies, and were going to take up the cage of mice and go out," Jimmy explained, "the fire engine came past, and Ted and I ran out to see it and we went to the fire, but it wasn't a big one, and we forgot about the mice; didn't we, Teddy?"

"Yes," said Teddy, "we did. And I didn't think about 'em until a little while ago, 'cause we started to play marbles, and—and—"

"Yes, and by your thoughtlessness you have made a lot of trouble," Mr. Martin remarked. "I am sorry for this, Teddy. If many more things happen I shall have to get rid of Uncle Toby's pets."

"Oh, don't do that!" begged the little Curlytop boy. "I'll put the rats and mice back in the cage and I'll fasten the door so they can't get out again. Don't send Uncle Toby's animals away, Daddy! We want to have a circus with them!"

"And I'll help pay for the buns the rats ate," added Jimmy. "It was partly my fault for making Ted forget."

"Oh, no, I can't allow that," said Mr. Martin, "though it is very good of you to offer, Jimmy. I will pay Mr. Capper for the buns the rats ate, and after this Teddy must be more careful."

"Can we take away the buns and cookies the mice didn't eat?" asked the little Curlytop chap, as he and his chum began picking up the pets and putting them back in the cage. The animals were tame and did not mind being handled.

"Take away all the buns in the window! They are of no more use to me!" exclaimed the baker. "But, Mr. Martin, I will not charge you full price for the things—only what it cost to make them. For, as you say, it was an advertisement. And I know the boys did not mean it."

"Indeed we didn't!" cried Teddy. "We can take the broken buns and feed them to Skyrocket and Top, and Mr. Nip and Jack will eat them, too," he said to his father. "It will be just as good as buying stale bread for the monkey and the parrot, Daddy. I guess they'll like buns better."

"I shouldn't be surprised if they did," laughed Mr. Martin. "Well, as you say, Teddy, it will save buying stale bread." Some of the pets were fed on this, and now the broken buns would take its place for a few meals.

By this time the crowd began leaving the bakery, as the excitement was over. Teddy and Jimmy picked up the last of the rats and mice, putting them back in the mended cage.

"And make sure the door of the cage is fastened," Mr. Martin said to Teddy, as the baker was paid for the buns. "We don't want the creatures getting loose again."

"It's good and tight," Teddy said. "They won't get out again except when we take them out to do circus tricks."

Carrying the cage of white mice and rats between them, Teddy and Jimmy walked down the street in front of Mr. Martin, and soon the pets were safely back in the barn.

"I'm a crack-crack-cracker!" cried the green, red and yellow parrot, as the boys entered. The talkative bird whistled, at which sound Skyrocket and Top, who were asleep in one corner of the barn, awakened and began to bark loudly.

"Your parrot whistles just like one of us fellows," said Jimmy to Teddy.

"Yes, he does," admitted the Curlytop chap. "I have been trying to think what tricks we could make him do in the circus. But the trouble is he doesn't always talk or whistle when you want him to. And when you don't want him to he nearly always does it."

"Well, anyway, he'll be nice to look at in the pet circus," said Jimmy. "And in the regular circus they have animals and birds to look at, as well as the kind that do tricks."

"Yes," agreed Teddy, "I guess so."

"I'm a crack-crack-cracker!" shrieked the parrot again, pulling himself up to the top of his cage by means of his big beak, his black tongue licking the bars as if he liked them.

"Well, if you're a crack-crack-cracker, here's a bun-bun-bunner for you," laughed Teddy, and out of the bag Mr. Martin had carried from the bakeshop Teddy took several of the broken pieces and fed them to the parrot.

Seeing this, Jack, the monkey, who was in his cage, set up a chattering such as he must have learned in the jungle where he came from.

"What's the matter with him?" Jimmy wanted to know.

"I guess he wants some of the broken buns, too," said Teddy. "Here, you give the monkey some, and I'll feed Skyrocket and Top. They want some, too."

Soon such of Uncle Toby's pets as liked this form of food were having all the buns they wanted. Mr. Nip, the parrot, tore his pieces of the buns apart to get at the currants. But Jack, Top and Skyrocket ate theirs down, currants and all, as if they liked every crumb.

The white rats and mice were not given any of the broken buns, as it was thought they had had enough in the bakery, and Teddy knew it was not wise to overfeed any pet animals.

Cats, dogs and other pets should not be fed too much, though of course they should not be allowed to go hungry very long. When animals can run around as they please, or when they live wild in the jungle or forest, they never eat too much. They know when to stop. But often persons, wishing to be kind, will give their dogs and cats too much meat, or other rich food. And as these pets do not run around and exercise very much, they cannot digest all they eat, so they often become ill. Teddy did not want this to happen to any of his pets.

Another thing he was careful about was always to see that they had plenty of fresh water. Nothing is more important than this. It is cruel to have any pet suffer for water to drink, especially in summer. So if you keep pets of any kind, don't feed them too much, but give them plenty of water. They never can take too much of this.

"When you going to have your circus?" asked Jimmy of Teddy, when the animals had quieted down, eating the pieces of buns.

"Oh, pretty soon, I guess. Janet and I are going to teach them a lot of new tricks."

"I wish I could help," said Jimmy.

"You can," Teddy promised. "Jan and I will need someone to help us with the circus. I'm going to ask Jack Turton and Harry Kent, too. Jack is so funny and fat he'll make a good clown."

"I'd rather be one of the animal trainers," said Jimmy.

"That's what you and I'll be—animal trainers," decided Teddy. "My sister Jan's good with animals, too. She isn't afraid of even a snake."

"That's good," decided Jimmy. "Maybe we could get some snakes to have in the circus—little ones, you know."

"It would be fine!" exclaimed Teddy. "But where can we get any?"

"Oh, in the woods, I guess. I'll see if I can find any. But I've got to go home now."

"All right. Come over to-morrow and we'll start training the animals," replied Teddy.

And the next day Teddy, Janet and Jimmy began to teach the pets some new tricks. I will tell you about them when the time comes. It was not easy work, and more than once the Curlytops and their friend were discouraged. For just when they thought they had Top and Skyrocket so they would do a trick together, one or the other of the dogs would run away, wagging his tail, however, in friendly fashion, to show there were no hard feelings.

The cats were the hardest to teach. Snuff did very well with his ball rolling trick and one or two others, and Turnover would turn in a sort of side-somersault whenever told to do so by Janet. But to teach the two cats to do tricks together was much harder.

It was this—the tricks they could do together—that made Tip and Top such a valuable team of dogs.

"Do you think you'll ever get Tip back?" asked Jimmy, as he, with the Curlytops, was resting one day after putting the pets through some of their tricks.

"We keep hoping so," said Janet.

"But it doesn't look so now," added her brother. "He's been gone so long, and not even the police can find him. They can't find Shorty, either. I guess Shorty and Tip ran a way together."

"And maybe Shorty has Tip in a circus, making him do tricks," added Janet.

"Maybe," agreed Teddy. "But now we've got to think where

we're going to get a tent for our show. If we give a pet animal circus we've got to have a tent."

"Sure!" agreed Jimmy. "It wouldn't be a circus without a tent. But maybe my father can get us one. He used to be in the army."

"Oh, let's go ask him!" cried Janet. "We can leave our pets here in the barn now, for they've been fed and watered."

Off the children hurried to Jimmy's house. His father was not at home, but Mrs. Norton said she thought her husband could get a tent that would do for the circus.

"And since you have been feeding the animals, wouldn't you like to feed yourselves now?" asked Jimmy's mother, with a smile at the Curlytops and her own son.

"Feed ourselves—how?" asked Teddy. At the same time he noticed a most delicious smell coming from Mrs. Norton's kitchen.

"I have just baked some molasses cookies," went on Jimmy's mother, "and I have some lovely, cool milk. Would you like some glasses of milk and molasses cookies?"

"Sure!" exclaimed Teddy.

"Fine!" cried Jimmy.

"We'd like it very much, if you please," said Janet, and she was extra polite, to make up for the rather boisterous manner in which Teddy spoke. But the boys meant to be polite and, after all, that is what counts.

Soon the Curlytops and their friend were out on the side

porch, drinking the cool, rich milk and eating the fresh molasses cookies. It was while they were thus sitting, talking about the circus they were going to give, that into the yard came running Top, Uncle Toby's trick dog.

"Hello, Top!" called Teddy. "Were you looking for us?"

Top barked and wagged his tail. Then he acted in a strange manner. He ran up to Teddy, and caught hold of the boy's coat.

"Oh, he's trying to bite you!" exclaimed Janet.

"He is not! Top would never bite me!" declared Teddy. But he wondered what the dog was trying to do.

Then Top let go his hold of the coat, and ran a little way toward the gate. There he stopped and looked back toward the children.

"What makes him act that funny way?" asked Jimmy.

"I don't know," answered Teddy.

With another bark, and wagging his tail, Top again ran up to Teddy and pulled on his coat.

"I know what it is!" exclaimed the Curlytop boy. "Something has happened, and Top has come to tell us and get us to go with him! Come on, Jimmy! Come on, Jan!"

CHAPTER XII

MR. NIP'S ALARM

Together the two Curlytops and their friend Jimmy Norton ran out of Jimmy's yard and down the street, following Top, the trick dog. For as soon as Top had seen that Teddy was following after him, which, evidently, was just what Top wanted, the dog raced on, barking wildly.

"Do you think he came to call you?" panted Janet, as she ran beside her brother.

"Sure he did," Ted answered. "Didn't you ever read in books how dogs do that when they want you to come to help somebody who's in trouble—like somebody in the water?"

"I've read lots of stories like that," said Jimmy.

"Oh, maybe something has happened to Trouble!" cried Janet.

"Mother took Trouble down town with her," Teddy answered. "So if Trouble is in trouble Top wouldn't know it."

"Maybe our house is on fire," went on Janet, who seemed quite determined to have something dreadful happen.

"You'd hear the alarm bell and see the engines if there was a fire," declared Jimmy.

"Well, it's *something*!" exclaimed Janet. "Isn't it a pity dogs can't talk like parrots? If they could, Top could tell us just what the matter was."

"We'll see pretty soon," said her brother. "We're almost at our house, and it must be there that something is the matter."

As the children were racing down the street, with Top running in front of them, looking back every now and then to make sure the Curlytops and Jimmy were following, a man stopped the children and said:

"Why are you chasing that poor dog? Don't you know it is wrong to tease and annoy animals?"

"We're not teasing him," Teddy answered. "He's our dog, anyhow."

"That is no matter," the fussy man said. "I think it is wrong to chase dogs or to tie tin cans on their tails."

"As if we'd tie a tin can to the tail of our nice Top!" exclaimed Janet. "We *never* tie cans to dogs' tails!" she added. "And we're running after Top because he wants us to. He came to get us because something has happened at our house."

Seeing that the children had stopped, because the strange man had halted them, Top came running back, barking and wagging his tail. He caught hold of Teddy's coat, and again pulled it.

"See!" exclaimed Ted. "He wants us to follow him. He did

that before, and that's why we ran after him, not because we're chasing him, Mister."

The man looked at the excited dog and at the kind-faced children. He must have known they would never have harmed animals, for he said:

"Oh, excuse me! I guess I made a mistake. I thought you were chasing the poor dog. Excuse me!"

The strange man turned and hurried off down the street, and after looking toward him for a few seconds the Curlytops and their chum again hastened along, following Top, who grew more excited all the while.

Into the yard of the Martin house dashed Top, closely followed by the children. But the dog did not stop at the house, nor did he run toward the barn where the other pets were kept. When Ted, Janet and Jimmy went over to Jimmy's house they had left the two dogs and the two cats playing outside the barn. Now there was no sight of Snuff and Turnover, nor of Skyrocket, the other dog.

Down past the barn and toward the brook into which Trouble had more than once fallen, ran Top, the trick dog.

"Oh, Trouble must have come back and have fallen in!" cried Janet.

"I don't believe so," said her brother. "If Trouble was in the water you'd hear him howling."

"Unless his head was under," suggested Jimmy.

"Yes, unless his head under," agreed Teddy. "But I don't believe it's Trouble. If it was anything like that, Top wouldn't come all the way to your house after us, Jimmy. He'd have barked and have gotten someone around here to come to the rescue."

"There isn't anybody home at our house but us, and we weren't home," explained Janet. "Mother and Trouble are down town, and Susan, our new girl, has gone out."

"I guess that's why Top came to us," Teddy said. "But where is he going, anyhow, and what is the matter?"

Barking and still wagging his tail, to show how glad he was that the children were coming where he wanted them, Top led the way down along the brook. The Curlytops passed the place where they had played ships the day Trouble was sent afloat in the box—the day Uncle Toby's letter came, telling about the pets he was leaving.

"What is it, Top? What's the matter, old fellow?" asked Teddy.

A bark was the dog's answer. But a moment later, as the children turned a bend in the stream, they heard a howl coming from a bunch of tall cat-tail plants growing on the edge of a swamp not far from the brook. It was the mournful howl of a dog in pain.

"That's Skyrocket!" cried Teddy.

"And he's in trouble!" added Janet.

"And that's why Top came to get us," declared Jimmy.

Top was barking louder than ever now, and as the Curlytops and their friend hurried along they could hear, more plainly, the howls of the dog they felt sure was their own, dear Skyrocket.

And a moment later, as they parted the green spears of the cat-tails, they saw, lying on the ground in the mud and water, poor Skyrocket. Their pet looked up at them and howled mournfully.

"Oh, he's drowning!" cried Janet, as she saw that Skyrocket was partly covered by the water of the swamp.

"He's got a broken leg!" said Jimmy.

"Dogs can go on three legs, if one is broken, though they can't go very fast," said Teddy. "Skyrocket is caught fast, that's what's the matter."

Top seemed overjoyed that he had brought help to his dog friend. Close up beside Skyrocket Top crawled, whining in sympathy, and then Top began licking, with his red tongue, one of Skyrocket's legs.

"Oh, I see what the matter is!" cried Teddy. "Skyrocket's leg is caught in a trap! That's why he couldn't get loose! Look!"

Teddy pointed to where, half hidden in the mud, water, and grass, was a spring trap. It was fast to a chain, and the chain was attached to a wooden stake, driven into the ground. But, worst of all, the steel jaws of the trap had snapped shut on the lower part of Skyrocket's left hind leg. The poor dog tried to stand up, but could not, as whenever he attempted to move the chain held him back.

"Poor Skyrocket!" murmured Janet, almost ready to cry.

"I'll get him loose!" said Teddy.

"It's a good thing Top came and told us what the matter was, or maybe we'd never have known it," remarked Jimmy.

"Come on, Jim! Help me open the trap and get Sky's leg out," said Teddy. "You pat his head—I mean Sky's head, Jan, and that will let him know we aren't going to hurt him."

So while Top looked on, whining in sympathy with his injured dog friend, and while Janet softly rubbed the head of Skyrocket, the two boys opened the trap. While Jimmy held it steady Teddy stepped on the strong spring with his foot. This was the only way to open it.

In another moment the trap was gently pulled loose from the leg of Skyrocket, and the poor dog, with a whine of thanks, managed to stand up. He tried to step on the injured leg, but quickly drew it up with a howl of pain.

"Oh, maybe it's broken!" half sobbed Janet.

"A dog can get well with a broken leg, but a horse can't," said Jimmy. "At least a horse never does, because he is so big he can't be kept off his leg until it heals. A horse can't go on three legs like a dog."

"A horse can stand up on two legs, and walk a little. I've seen 'em in a circus!" declared Janet. "But I never saw a horse go on three legs."

"There goes Skyrocket on three legs!" called Teddy, for his pet hobbled along a little way, to a drier part of the swamp, and then lay down and began licking with his red tongue the leg that had been caught in a trap.

"Look and see if it's broken," suggested Jimmy. "If it is, we'd better tie sticks around it like the principal of our school did one day when Tommy Hicks broke his leg."

"I remember that time," responded Teddy. "Easy now, old fellow," he said to Skyrocket. "Let me feel your leg to see if it is broken."

Gently, very gently, Teddy moved his fingers along the injured leg. Skyrocket whined a little, but remained lying there quietly. At last Teddy stood up.

"I don't believe it's broken," he said. "I guess it was only pinched hard in the trap."

"It's a smooth-jawed trap, not the kind with the teeth like a saw," said Jimmy, looking at the trap which had been allowed to spring shut after Skyrocket's leg was drawn out. "They use big traps, with terrible sharp teeth and jaws, to catch bears," said the little boy.

"I'm glad this wasn't that kind of trap," said Janet. "But who put it here, anyhow?"

"It's an old one, and rusty," went on Jimmy, looking at the trap, while Teddy got some water from the swamp in the top of his cap, and poured it over the bruised place where Skyrocket's leg seemed to hurt most. The water appeared to ease the pain a little, and the dog whined gratefully. Top, now that his work of bringing someone to the rescue was over, stretched out in a cool place and rested, breathing with his mouth open and his tongue hanging out. This is the way dogs always cool themselves.

"Yes, it's an old, rusty trap," agreed Teddy, coming up to look at the thing that had caught Skyrocket. "I guess some muskrat hunter left it here, all set and ready to catch some animal that came along, ever since last winter. Maybe the spring was rusty, and not so strong, and that's why it didn't break Skyrocket's leg."

"I'm glad it didn't!" voiced Janet.

"So'm I," echoed Jimmy. "But how are you going to get Skyrocket home?"

"Oh, it isn't far, and he can go on three legs," said Teddy. "Come on, old fellow," he called, and Skyrocket managed to hobble along the brook path and up to the house. Top walked along beside him, every now and then putting out his tongue and gently licking his companion.

"He's kissing him 'cause he's sorry," observed Janet.

"We're all sorry," declared Teddy. "I'm going to ask mother if we can't have the animal doctor look at Skyrocket's leg."

"Why, children! what is the matter? Has anything happened, Curlytops?" asked Mrs. Martin, who had reached home with Trouble by the time the two boys and Janet made their way up the back path to the house.

"Skyrocket's leg was caught in a trap, and can't we have the animal doctor see if it's broken?" Teddy asked.

Then the story was told, not forgetting the brave and intelligent part played by Top, and Mrs. Martin examined Skyrocket's sore leg.

"I don't believe it is broken, but we'll have the doctor look to make sure," she said.

And you can just imagine how glad the Curlytops were, and Jimmy also, when the doctor said:

"The leg is not broken, but it is badly bruised. However, it will be well in a week or so. Keep Skyrocket as quiet as you can."

"We will!" promised Janet.

"We want him to get well so he can be in the circus," added Teddy.

"Oh, I guess he'll be all right for that," said the doctor, with a laugh as he hurried away to look after a sick horse.

A soft bed was made for Skyrocket in the barn, and a basin of fresh water was placed near him. He licked Teddy's hands in gratitude as the little boy patted him in coming away.

It was several days after the adventure with Skyrocket and the trap that something else exciting happened at the home of the Curlytops.

Mr. Nip, the red, green and yellow parrot, became ill. His feathers were ruffled up, he sat all in a lump on his perch, and he would not eat.

"I guess you'd better have the man from the bird store come up to see your parrot," said Mr. Martin, when he went out to the barn at the children's request to look at Mr. Nip. "Your mother will call the bird man on the telephone."

And when the bird man—that is to say the man who kept the bird and fish store—came to see Mr. Nip, he said the parrot should be kept in the kitchen and fed special food with a little medicine in it for a few days.

So that is how it happened that Mr. Nip was moved in from the barn to the house. And it was the third night that the parrot had slept in the house that something happened.

In the middle of the night the Curlytops were awakened by hearing Mr. Nip cry out loudly:

"Go 'way! Go 'way! I'm a crack-crack-cracker! Get out of here!"

Teddy and Janet, who seemed to be the only ones awakened by this alarm of Mr. Nip, listened, half shivering in their beds.

"Did you hear that?" called Teddy to his sister in the next room.

"Yes. What is it?" inquired Janet.

"It's Mr. Nip," whispered back the Curlytop boy. "He's calling to someone. Maybe daddy or mother's down there giving him medicine."

But just then the parrot set up such a screeching as the children had never heard, since he came from Uncle Toby's at least.

"Go 'way! Go 'way!" cried the bird. "I'm a crack-crack-cracker! Police! Fire! Burglars!"

And then, to the surprise and terror of the Curlytops, a strange voice, somewhere downstairs in their house, exclaimed in a harsh whisper:

"Do something to that parrot! Throw a rug over his cage, or he'll have the whole house awake. Make him be quiet!"

CHAPTER XIII

THE HAND-ORGAN MAN

The Curlytops cuddled down in their beds. Janet said afterward that she pulled the clothes over her ears. Teddy did the same at first, and then he began to think. And his first thought was that someone besides those who had a right to be there, were in his mother's kitchen. And of course the next thought that came to Teddy was:

"Burglars!"

Somehow or other he happened to hit on just exactly the very thing that was happening downstairs.

"Jan! Janet!" hoarsely whispered Teddy, thrusting his head out from under the sheet he had pulled over himself.

But Janet did not answer.

From down in the kitchen, however, the little Curlytop boy could plainly hear the parrot saying:

"I'm a crack-crack-cracker!"

"I'll hit him a crack if he doesn't keep quiet!" said a harsh

Howard R. Garis

voice. "Do you hear anyone coming, Bill?"

"No," replied another voice, which, Teddy thought, must belong to the man called Bill.

"They're burglars trying to get our parrot!" quickly thought Teddy. "I'm not going to let them have Mr. Nip. If they take him away he can't be in our circus. Course he can't do tricks like Skyrocket and Top, but he's nice to look at. The burglars shan't get Mr. Nip!"

Teddy slipped out of bed and went, as softly as he could, to the room where his father and mother slept. They were sound in slumber, which is the reason neither of them heard the parrot talking and screeching. Besides, the rooms of Teddy and Janet were nearer the kitchen.

"Daddy! Mother! Wake up!" whispered Teddy.

The sound of his parents' heavy breathing was the only answer the little boy received.

"Daddy! Mother!" he called again. "Wake up! There's a burglar downstairs, and he's trying to take Mr. Nip!"

There was silence for a moment, and then Teddy reached over and gently pulled his mother by her hand, which was hanging down outside the bed.

"What is it? What's the matter?" suddenly asked Mrs. Martin. In another instant she had pulled the cord attached to an electric light over her bed, and the room was bright in a moment. Then Mr. Martin awakened, and both parents looked at the little Curlytop boy.

"What's the matter, Ted? Walking in your sleep?" asked his

father. For sometimes Teddy did do that.

In answer the little fellow put his finger to his lips to make his father and mother understand that he wanted them to keep quiet.

"It's burglars—two of 'em!" whispered Teddy. "One is named Bill, but I don't know the other one's name. They've come to get Mr. Nip."

"What's that—our parrot? Nonsense!" exclaimed Mr. Martin. "You have been dreaming, Teddy, my boy. Go back to bed."

But just then, from down in the kitchen, came the voice of the parrot shrieking:

"I'm a crack-crack-cracker! Police, Fire! Burglars!"

Then came a banging, clashing sound, and a man's voice cried:

"There! See if that will keep you quiet!"

An instant later there was a sound as if the parrot's cage had been knocked over, or had tumbled over, and Mr. Nip cried:

"Help! Help! Help!"

Out of bed jumped Mr. Martin, going toward the closet where he kept his revolver.

"It is burglars!" he whispered.

"Oh, you mustn't go down! They might shoot you! Go to the window and call the police!" begged Mrs. Martin, clinging to her husband.

Mr. Martin did both. He went to the window and fired a shot from his revolver up into the air. My! what a loud noise it made, and it set Skyrocket and Top to barking out in the barn. Perhaps the monkey chattered also, but he could not be heard. However, Mr. Nip's shrill shrieking seemed to resound all over the neighborhood.

There was a moon, and as he looked from his bedroom window Mr. Martin, by its light, saw two men running out of the side gate.

"There go the burglars!" he cried, and again he fired a shot. This made the strange men run all the faster, and by this time Trouble had awakened and was crying.

"Janet, you come in and stay with Trouble," called Mrs. Martin "I'll get dressed, and then, when the police come, we must see what the burglars have taken! Oh, what a dreadful night! I hope they haven't stolen much!"

"And I hope they didn't take Mr. Nip," echoed Teddy.

"I don't believe they carried away much of anything," Mr. Martin remarked, as he slipped on his bath robe. "I didn't see them carry much as they ran."

By this time Janet had gone in to Trouble, comforting him, stopping his frightened sobs, and telling him a little story. And then several neighbors, roused by Mr. Martin's shooting, came in, and a little later the police arrived.

An examination was made in the kitchen, and it was found that the burglars had broken open a window and had thus come into the house. But no sooner had they entered than Mr. Nip roused up and began to talk. And it was his talk and his loud voice that had awakened Janet and Teddy.

The burglars, fearing the parrot would awaken someone, had tried to silence him by throwing something over the cage. But the bird, who was always more excited when strangers were around, kept on screeching and yelling. Then one of the burglars, in his anger, must have thrown something at the parrot's cage, knocking it over, and this was one of the crashes heard upstairs.

"Poor Mr. Nip!" said Teddy, when he was allowed to come down with his father and mother. The parrot's cage was set upright again, no damage having been done.

The excitement seemed to have made Mr. Nip feel better, for he showed no signs of illness as he cried again and again:

"Police! Fire! Burglars! I'm a crack-crack-cracker!"

"You're a good polly!" declared Mrs. Martin. "You saved our house from being robbed!"

And there is no question but what Mr. Nip had done that. Bringing the sick parrot into the kitchen had been the means of scaring away the burglars. No thieves will stay in a house at night if they hear someone moving around, or hear voices, and these bad men may have thought at first that Mr. Nip was some real person, calling for the police.

At any rate the burglars ran away, not getting anything that they came to steal. And it was all due to Mr. Nip.

"He'll sure be in our circus now," said Teddy, as he made ready to go back to bed again, the neighbors and police having left. "Everybody will want to see a parrot that drove away two burglars, won't they, Daddy?"

"They probably will, Teddy boy," his father replied. "Well,

one of Uncle Toby's pets has more than paid for his board bill by to-night's work."

"Aren't you glad we got 'em?" asked Teddy.

"Yes, I guess I am," his father answered, laughing.

"Say! I wish I'd been over to your house last night," exclaimed Jimmy Norton to Teddy, when the story of the attempt to rob was being talked over among the children.

"Well, I was wishing I was somewhere else," said Janet. "Oh, but I was scared!"

"I was at first, but I knew I had to tell my mother or my father," remarked Teddy. "So I got out of bed."

"Teddy was brave," declared Janet.

"Oh, that wasn't anything," the little Curlytop boy said modestly. "I wasn't as brave as Mr. Nip. He called the burglars names!"

"Everybody will be glad to come to the circus to see him," said Harry Kent, who was going to help with the show.

"We'll put Mr. Nip in a special cage, and put a sign on so people will know he's the parrot that scared the burglars," suggested fat Jackie Turton.

In fact, Mr. Nip became quite celebrated. For there was an account in the newspaper of the attempted burglary at the Martin house, and the part the parrot had played was well told, so that all over Cresco Mr. Nip was talked about.

"It's a good advertisement for our circus, isn't it, Daddy?"

asked Teddy, for the paper mentioned that the Curlytops had a number of pets they were getting ready to place on exhibition in a show.

"Yes," said Mr. Martin, "it is."

"What are you going to do with the money you get from your circus—if you get any?" asked Mrs. Martin of the Curlytops one day about a week after the burglars had gotten in. By this time Mr. Nip was quite well again, and could go back to the barn to be with the monkey, the alligator and the white mice and the rats.

"Oh, we'll get *some* money," declared Teddy. "But I don't know what we'll do with it. Maybe we'll buy more pets."

"Oh, I hope not!" laughed his mother. "You have enough now."

As the days passed the Curlytops and their friends worked with Uncle Toby's animals, teaching them several new tricks. More than once Teddy and Janet wished they had Tip, the missing dog, as he had performed so well with Top. But no word had come about him, and it was felt he was gone forever.

"Skyrocket is good," Teddy told his boy chums, "but he isn't as good a trick dog as Tip and Top were when they did their tricks together."

"Maybe we can teach Jack, the monkey, some new tricks," suggested Harry Kent.

"Oh, yes, Jack must learn a lot of tricks," agreed Teddy. "We'll start on him now, I guess, as about the only tricks Snuff can do are to roll around on the football and jump through a paper hoop."

That last trick was a new one, and really had not been intended for Snuff. One day Teddy and Janet were getting some paper-covered hoops ready for Skyrocket or Top to jump through, as the dogs seemed to like that trick. Snuff and Turnover were playing together near by, and when Turnover chased Snuff, the Persian cat leaped right through a paper hoop.

"Oh, if we could only make him do that for the circus!" Janet cried. "It would be great!"

"We'll try," Teddy had said. And, after many trials, they did succeed in getting Snuff to leap through a paper hoop. It was a fine trick.

But now the Curlytops planned to teach Jack, their monkey, some tricks in addition to a few that he had learned from Uncle Toby or the sailor. So Jack was brought out from his cage and given a banana, fruit of which he was very fond.

"What trick shall we teach him?" asked Janet.

"I think a jumping trick would be good," Teddy answered. "I'll go and get some boxes, and we'll make a high thing, like a tower, of them. We'll get Jack up on top, and have him jump down. That will be great, won't it?"

"Fine," agreed Janet. "I'll help you get the boxes."

The Curlytops left their monkey sitting on a bench in the yard while they went back into the barn after the boxes. Jack was peacefully eating his banana when Teddy and Janet left him. But when the children came out with the boxes, it having taken longer to find them than they had thought, Jack was not to be seen.

"Oh, Jack is gone!" cried Janet, looking around.

"Maybe he's up in a tree," suggested Teddy. "Here, Jack! Jack!" he called.

But there was no chattering answer, and the monkey was not to be found. He had not gone back into the barn, where the other pets were, and Trouble, who was playing in the back yard, said Jack had not passed him.

"Where can he be?" asked Janet. She and Teddy were beginning to worry, when Mrs. Johnson, into whose baby carriage Slider had once been put by Baby William, called from across the street:

"Are you looking for your dog, children?"

"No'm. For our monkey," answered Teddy.

"Oh, maybe the hand-organ man has him," said Mrs. Johnson. "I saw an Italian with an organ go into your yard a little while ago."

"Did he have a monkey with him?" asked Teddy.

"I don't much believe that he did. I saw the man go in, but I didn't notice a monkey. But I remember now that when the organ man came out, he had a monkey with him. Maybe it was yours."

"I'm sure it was!" cried Janet. "Oh, Ted! The hand-organ man has taken Jack! He took Jack when we were in the barn!"

Howard R. Garis

"I didn't hear any hand-organ music," Teddy said.

"Course he wouldn't play when he came to get Jack!" exclaimed Jan, with tears in her eyes. "Oh, Ted, go for the police! The hand-organ man has taken our monkey! Oh dear!"

CHAPTER XIV

TURNOVER AND SKYROCKET

Perhaps it would have been better for the Curlytops to have run into the house and have told their mother about the missing monkey. But neither Janet nor Teddy thought of this, because they were so excited over the news that Mrs. Johnson gave them—the news that Jack had been taken away by a hand-organ man.

"We've got to get him back!" cried Teddy.

"Of course!" agreed Janet. "It won't be half a circus without a monkey in it."

"Come on!" called Ted, and out of the yard he ran, followed by Janet. The Curlytops took one look to make sure that Trouble was safe before going away and leaving him. The little fellow was playing with Turnover and Skyrocket. He would do that for a long time.

Out of the yard and down the street ran the little boy and girl, thinking only of getting their monkey back.

"Did he go this way?" Teddy called to Mrs. Johnson, who was watching him and his sister.

Howard R. Garis

"Yes, right down that street," answered the mother of Baby Ruth. "But you had better not chase after him. He might not give Jack back to you, and he might be cross, and maybe it wasn't your monkey he had at all, Curlytops!"

But Teddy and Janet did not stay to hear all this. They hurried on, Teddy a little ahead of his sister, because, being a boy and a year older, he could go faster. But every now and then he stopped to wait for her. They turned the corner of a street, and Teddy, being in the lead, had the first glimpse down it.

"Do you see him?" gasped Janet, hurrying up to the side of her brother.

"No, he isn't here," was the answer.

Mr. Anderson, who left groceries at the home of the Curlytops, came along just then in the delivery wagon.

"Whoa!" he called to his horse. And then, seeing that Teddy and Janet were worried about something, he asked them: "Have you lost your little brother?" Mr. Anderson knew how often Trouble ran away.

"No, sir," answered Teddy. "We're looking for our monkey."

"And the hand-organ man," added Janet.

"Monkey? Hand-organ man?" exclaimed Mr. Anderson. "Are you going to give a party, and do you want the hand-organ man to play at it, and the monkey to do tricks?"

"Oh, no, this is our own pet monkey," exclaimed Janet.

"The hand-organ man took him away when he was eating a

banana," added Teddy.

"Our monkey—his name is Jack—he was eating the banana —not the hand-organ man," said Jan, fearing Mr. Anderson might not understand what her brother meant.

"And he does tricks, and we're going to have him in our little circus—I mean our monkey does tricks," went on Teddy.

"Well, I guess I'll get the straight of it after a while," said Mr. Anderson, with a little laugh. "Anyhow it seems that some stray hand-organ man has taken your monkey, has he?"

"Yes. And we want our monkey back!" cried Janet.

"Then you'd better get up here in the wagon with me," went on the grocery man, "and I'll drive you down the street. It will be quicker than walking, and, as I've delivered all the orders, I'm in no hurry to get back to the store. Hop up, Curlytops!"

He helped Janet and Teddy to the seat beside him, and drove off. It was not the first time the children had ridden with Mr. Anderson, for he often took them with him when he had occasion to stop at their house.

"Do you know which street he went down?" asked the grocery man, as he called to his brown horse which started off again.

"We don't know," answered Teddy. "We didn't see him. We were in the barn, getting some boxes so Jack—that's the monkey—could do some tricks. We left him eating a banana, and when we came out he was gone. But Mrs. Johnson said she saw a hand-organ man come out of our yard and he had a monkey."

Howard R. Garis

"And it must 'a' been Jack!" added Janet.

"Well, we'll try to get him back for you," promised Mr. Anderson, as he guided the horse down the street. "And we'll ask some of the people we meet if they have seen Jack."

"Oh, now I know we'll get him back!" exclaimed Janet, and there was a smile on her face where, before, there had been a sad look, which always came just before she cried. "I'm glad we met you, Mr. Anderson," she said.

"So am I," agreed Teddy.

The first person they met was Patrick, the man who worked for Mrs. Blake, the lady into whose house Jack made his way one night, making Mrs. Blake think he was a fuzzy burglar.

"Oh, Patrick!" cried Teddy, "a hand-organ man took our monkey away. Have you seen him?"

"Which? The hand-organ man or the monkey?" asked Mrs. Blake's gardener.

"Either one," said Janet. "He's the same monkey that was once in your house, you know."

"Yes," returned Patrick, with a smile, "I know. Well, I'm sorry, but I didn't see either the hand-organ man or the monkey."

"Giddap!" called Mr. Anderson to his horse. "We must try someone else."

They drove along a little farther, and next they met Sam White, a colored man, who cut grass and did other work for the neighbors of the Curlytops.

"Oh, Sam! have you seen our monkey, Jack?" called Teddy.

"Seen a monkey? No'm, I hasn't," answered the colored man, who had been wheeling a lawn-mower.

"Did you see a hand-organ man?" asked Janet.

"Yes'm, I done seen a hand-organ man," was the answer. "He's jest 'round de corner ob de next street. But I didn't see him hab no monkey."

"Maybe he has our monkey hidden inside the hand-organ so no one will see Jack!" cried Teddy. "Please hurry, Mr. Anderson!"

"I will," promised the grocery man. "Giddap there, Molasses!" he called to his horse. "We're in a hurry!"

And as they turned the corner of the street, toward which Sam White had pointed, there came to the ears of the Curlytops the strains of hand-organ music.

"There he is! I see him!" cried Janet, pointing. "He's stopped, and he's playing!"

"Yes, and I see our monkey, too!" added Teddy. "Please hurry down there, Mr. Anderson, and we'll take Jack away from that bad hand-organ man."

"Maybe it isn't your monkey," said the grocer. "All monkeys look alike to me. I couldn't tell one from the other, but maybe you can. Giddap, Molasses!" he called again to his horse, and down the street clattered the Curlytops.

They came to a stop in front of the organ grinder just as the dark-colored Italian ground out the last strains of a tune. And there, surely enough, perched on the top of the organ, was a monkey.

"Jack! Jack! Come here!" cried Teddy, getting ready to jump down from his seat in the wagon.

"Come away from that bad man!" added Janet.

The organ grinder turned quickly, gave one look at the Curlytops and at Mr. Anderson, and then, slinging his organ up on his back, started hurriedly up the street, taking the monkey with him.

"Here! Hold on a minute!" called the grocer, getting down off the seat, and then helping Teddy and Janet down. "If you have a monkey belonging to these children you must give it back, or I'll call a policeman!"

"No! No!" jabbered the Italian. "Dis a-monk mine! Long time mine! No belong childerns! Goo'-bye!"

He would have been off down the street and around the corner in another few seconds, but Teddy, rushing after him, looked and made sure it really was Jack that the organ player had with him. There was a queer little tuft of white hair on the end of Jack's tail, and this monkey had the same mark.

"Jack! Jack!" cried Teddy. "Come on, to me! I'll give you all the bananas you want!"

"Dis-a my monk!" jabbered the Italian.

"He is not! He's ours!" declared Janet, as she hurried up to the side of her brother. "Make him give back our monkey that we got from Uncle Toby!" she appealed to Mr. Anderson.

"If he doesn't," said the grocer, "I'll call a policeman and—"

But just then Jack acted for himself. With a shrill chatter he broke loose from the string that was tied to the collar about his neck. There had been no cord on him when he was eating a banana in the yard of the Curlytops, and the hand-organ man must have tied it there after he took the children's pet. Once free, Jack made one leap and landed safe in Teddy's arms.

Now, Jack was rather a large monkey, and, jumping from a distance, as Jack did, he knocked Teddy over. Flat down on the sidewalk sat Teddy, the monkey clinging with its hairy arms about the little boy's neck.

"Oh! Oh!" exclaimed Janet, and then she stopped, for she did not know what else to say.

"Look out!" cried Mr. Anderson. "Maybe that's a savage monkey, and he'll bite you!"

"This is Jack all right," declared Teddy. "I know him and he knows me. He didn't hurt me. I—I just sat down, that's all," and the little Curlytop boy laughed.

Jack chattered, clung tighter to his master, and then the crowd that had gathered also laughed. For it looked so odd to see Teddy sitting on the sidewalk, with a monkey, quite a large one, clinging to his neck.

"What's the matter here? What's the trouble?" asked a gruff but not unkindly voice, and on the outside of the crowd appeared Policeman Cassidy.

"Oh, Cassidy," said Mr. Anderson, "this Italian took the Curlytops' monkey, and they just got him back—I mean they got the monkey back. The Italian—"

But with a half-smothered cry of anger, the Italian started to run down the street, his hand-organ swaying from side to side on his back. He had no wish to meet Policeman Cassidy and be arrested for having taken Jack.

And that is just what the Italian had done. He had sneaked into the yard and, seeing the monkey unfastened and eating a banana, had picked up the pet and hurried off with him. The Italian must have known how to talk to and handle monkeys, for Jack made no outcry, but went peaceably with his captor. Perhaps the monkey was afraid of being beaten. And, so that Jack could not get away, the Italian had tied a string to the collar.

But, thanks to Mr. Anderson and the grocery wagon, the Curlytops had gotten back their pet. The Italian had not played his organ very near the home of Teddy and Janet for fear of their hearing it, I suppose. But when he thought he was far enough away he started, and Sam White had heard him.

"Maybe the hand-organ man kept Jack hidden under his coat until he got down here," said Janet.

"Perhaps," agreed the grocer, as the crowd began to melt away, seeing there was to be no more excitement. "And now if you Curlytops, and your monkey, will get into the wagon, I'll drive you back home."

"Do you want me to chase after that Italian and arrest him?" asked the policeman.

"No, thank you, I guess not," answered Teddy, as he rubbed Jack's fuzzy head. "We got our monkey back, and now we can start to teach him some tricks for the circus. We'll send you a free ticket to the show, Mr. Anderson, 'cause you helped us get Jack back."

Janet whispered something to her brother.

"Oh, yes," added the little fellow, "we'd like to have you come, too, Mr. Policeman Cassidy."

"I'll come and stand guard at the ticket wagon," laughed the big, good-natured officer. "And if I see that Italian sneaking up I'll chase him."

"I guess he won't come," said Teddy. Then he and his sister climbed up on the seat beside Mr. Anderson and were driven back to their home. It was time, too, for their mother was out at the gate, holding Trouble by the hand, and looking up and down the street.

"Where have you been, Curlytops?" she asked them. "And what are you doing in Mr. Anderson's wagon—and with the monkey? Did Jack run away?" she asked.

"He was taken away," explained Teddy.

"By an old organ grinder," added Janet.

And then the story was told.

"Dear me," said Mrs. Martin, when it was finished. "I'm sure if your father and I had known all the things that were going to happen because of Uncle Toby's pets, we would not have brought them home."

"Oh, it's fun!" laughed Teddy, slipping down with Jack.

"And Policeman Cassidy is coming to our circus," said Janet.

"Don't forget me!" called Mr. Anderson, as he drove away with the wagon.

"We won't!" promised the Curlytops.

"You been take Jack to barber's?" asked Trouble, letting go his mother's hand to pat the monkey.

"The barber's?" repeated Teddy, as he put Jack down on a box and gave the pet a banana, as had been promised. "What made him think that?" Teddy asked his mother.

"He's been singing that Mother Goose verse, 'Barber, barber! shave a pig. How many hairs will make a wig? Four and twenty, that's enough, give the barber a pinch of snuff.' I suppose Trouble thought maybe Snuff, the cat, had something to do with a barber, and he got Jack mixed up in it somehow. But I am glad you Curlytops are home again. I was getting worried about you. What are you going to do now?"

"Teach Jack to jump off a high tower of boxes," explained Ted. "We were getting ready to do that when the Italian took Jack. Come on, Janet, we'll make the box tower."

"Me help!" cried Trouble.

"Oh, you'll be more bother than you will help," replied Janet. "You'll be knocking the tower over all the while, or trying to climb up on it. You go and play with Skyrocket and Turn-over," she advised, as the dog and cat came around the path.

"All wite! Me make Turn an' Sky do circus twicks!" said Trouble, talking half to himself.

Having made sure that Jack was comfortable and had not been harmed by the Italian who took him away, the Curlytops set about building, of old packing boxes, the tower off which they hoped their monkey would leap, thus doing a new trick for the pet circus. Teddy and Janet were so busy they paid no attention to Trouble, except to notice, now and then, that he was playing at the end of the yard with Skyrocket and Turnover, or "Sky" and "Turn", as he shortened the pets' names.

"There, I guess the tower is high enough for the first few jumps," Teddy remarked, as he nailed in place the last of the boxes. "We don't want Jack to jump down from too high a place at first."

"No," agreed Janet, "we don't. He might hurt himself, or he might get scared, and then he wouldn't want to be in the circus. But we ought to have some sort of net for him to jump into, didn't we ought, Teddy?"

"I guess we did," said the Curlytop boy. "Then we can make the tower higher. Oh, I know what we can have for a net!" he suddenly cried.

"What?" asked Janet.

Her brother pointed to a clothesline in the yard, across which were drying some lace curtains that had just been washed.

"They'll be just dandy for a circus net!" Teddy went on. "You can hold one end, and I'll hold the other. But we won't make the tower any higher for a while. I'll get a curtain for a net."

"S'pose mother will mind?" asked Janet.

"Oh, no, I don't s'pose so," answered Teddy. "It won't hurt the curtain. Jack isn't so big that he'll tear it, and if it gets dirty, an' maybe it will a little, we can wash it again. You get Jack now, and I'll get the curtain. Then we'll make Jack climb up to the top of the box tower and jump off."

"How you going to get him to go up?" asked Janet, when Ted came back with his mother's lace curtain which he had taken off the line.

"I'll put a piece of banana up there on the top box," Teddy answered. The pile of boxes, nailed together, was higher than his head, but he had brought out the stepladder so he could reach up with that.

"How you going to get Jack to jump down into the lace curtain net?" Janet went on.

"I'll hold out another piece of banana," Teddy replied. "Come on here, Jack, and learn a new trick!" he called to the monkey.

But just then both Teddy and Janet saw a sight that made them cry out in surprise. And the sight was that of Trouble, coming around the corner of the barn, driving before him Turnover and Skyrocket, the first cat and dog pets the Curlytops had ever owned. But Turnover and Skyrocket had never looked so funny as they did now, with Trouble urging them on and crying:

"I dot a new twick! I dot a new twick! Look what me make Turn an' Sky do!"

CHAPTER XV

PLANNING THE CIRCUS

"Well, look what that little tyke has done!" cried Teddy, with a laugh.

"All by himself, too!" added Janet. "How did he ever think of it?"

"And how he got Turnover and Skyrocket to stand still long enough to be harnessed up is a wonder!" said Teddy.

For that is what baby William had done. With bits of string, straps and strips torn from some pieces of cloth he had found in the barn, he had made a crazy jumble of a harness for the dog and the cat. They were tied and fastened together.

But this was not all. Besides harnessing the dog and cat together, like a team made up of a big horse and a little pony, Trouble had made the two pets fast to a small express wagon that he claimed as his very own, though it had once belonged to Teddy.

"And look what he has in the wagon!" cried Janet, now laughing as heartily as was Teddy. "My old rag doll—Miss Muffin!"

Howard R. Garis

In her earlier days Janet had a large rag doll, which had been named Miss Muffin, just why no one knew. But as she grew older and had other dolls, and finally had come to play more with her brother and the pets than with such toys, Janet had forgotten all about Miss Muffin. So the rag doll had been tossed here and there, sometimes in one corner and sometimes in another, getting more ragged, torn and dirty as the weeks went by.

But Baby William had found this old doll and had tied it to the little seat in his express wagon. And there sat Miss Muffin, one eye partly scratched off her painted cloth face, and the other eye, by some accident, skewed around until it was standing up and down, and did not lie sideways as most eyes do.

"I give Miss Muffin a wide," announced Trouble. "She 'ike it, an' maybe it's a twick for de circus!"

Teddy and Janet looked at one another and then they both laughed.

"Say, it *would* be a good trick!" said Teddy at length. "We could dress Trouble up funny like, and have him come in driving Turnover and Skyrocket. The people would clap like anything."

"I believe they would," agreed Janet.

"Did Turnover scratch you when you tied all those strings on, Trouble?" she asked her little brother.

"Nope! Turn, he 'ike it," declared Baby William. "An' Sky, he puts hims tongue on my hands and 'ick me."

"I guess he wouldn't have much trouble with Skyrocket,"

said Teddy. "I've harnessed the dog to little carts before. But I never hitched the dog and cat together. You made a fine trick there, Trouble."

"I be in circus?" asked the little fellow.

"Sure you may be in the circus," said Janet. "It will be one of the best acts. And we can tie ribbons on the necks of Sky and Turn, as Trouble calls them, to make it look prettier. Go on, Trouble," she said to her little brother, "let's see you drive 'em around the yard. Maybe they'll break away, or get all tangled up, and then it wouldn't be a good act for our show," she said to Teddy.

But Trouble seemed to have charmed Skyrocket and Turnover to do just what he wanted them to do, and they walked slowly around the paths in the yard, giving Miss Muffin a fine ride.

"Don't keep 'em hitched up too long, Trouble," advised Janet. "If you do they'll get tired, and won't like it next time."

"I undwess 'em now," said the little boy. By "undressing" he meant taking the string and strap harness off the dog and cat.

Turnover and Skyrocket seemed very glad to be set free, and they ran off together, while Trouble stayed with his brother and sister, as they had told him they were going to make Jack do a trick now.

It was time to see if they could get the monkey to do what was wanted of him. The tower of boxes had been built, and Teddy had two bananas, one to get Jack to climb up on top of the pile, and another yellow fruit to induce the monkey to leap down. The lace curtain net had also been provided.

"Now, Jack, we'll see what good you are," said Teddy, as he climbed up on the stepladder and placed the banana on the top-most box, letting part of the fruit stick out over the edge.

"Here, Jack!" called Teddy, standing half way up the ladder. "Come on and do your trick!"

The monkey chattered a little, but came to Teddy, who picked the fuzzy creature up in his arms. Holding Jack up, Teddy showed him the banana on top of the pile of boxes.

With another chatter, Jack scrambled out of Teddy's arms, and with the usual quickness of monkeys, was soon on top of the pile of boxes—the "tower" as Ted and Jan called it. When they gave their circus they planned to cover the pile of boxes with green boughs and pretend it was a big tree in the jungle.

"Oh, see!" cried Janet in delight, as she saw Jack on top of the pile, eating the banana he found there. "He's done the first part of the trick all right, Teddy!"

"Yes, and if he does the last part as well it will be fine!" declared the little Curlytop boy. "But the last is the hardest part. Jack may want to climb down instead of jumping. But first we'll let him eat the banana, and get hungry for the second one."

So the three children stood on the ground, and watched Jack, up on the tower, eating his banana. The monkey looked down, making funny faces, which he seemed to be doing most of the time, and Trouble laughed.

"He is funny!" laughed Janet. "I'm sure the people who come to our circus will like Jack."

"They'll like him a lot more if he does tricks," said Teddy. "Come on, Jan," he called, after a while. "We'll get the net ready now. I guess it's time he jumped for the other banana."

Mrs. Martin had not seen the Curlytops take her lace curtain off the line to use for a circus net. If she had, she would, of course, have stopped them. But Teddy and Janet did not think they were doing anything very wrong. As for Trouble, he never bothered his head about it. Whatever Ted or Janet did was all right to him.

"If we each have to hold one end of the curtain net, how are we going to hold out the banana so Jack will see it?" asked Janet of her older brother.

"We'll lay the banana in the middle of the net," decided Ted.

This was done, and when the curtain was held stretched as tightly as Janet and Teddy could pull it, as they had once seen the Cresco firemen stretch out a life-net in a practice drill, the banana was placed in the center.

"Come on now, Jack! Jump down!" called Teddy. "Jump down and get your other banana!"

Jack chattered, but did not jump. He clung to the edge of the tower of boxes, made two or three motions as if he were coming down, but he did not descend.

"I guess he doesn't see the banana," remarked Janet. "One of us ought to hold it up."

"We can't, and hold the net too," Teddy declared. "And if we don't hold the net, and Jack jumps, he may hurt himself, and then he can't be in the show."

"Oh, I know what we can do!" Janet declared.

"What?" asked Teddy.

"We can have Trouble hold the banana! Let him stand right near the outside edge of the net, near the middle, and hold up the banana. Then Jack will see it and jump."

"That is a good idea," remarked Teddy. He was always willing to give his sister credit for thinking of things to do. "Come on, Trouble," called Teddy to his brother. "Hold the banana up for Jack!"

"Eess, me do dat!" replied Baby William, so excited he could hardly talk at all, much less talk properly.

Eager to do his share in getting ready for the circus, Trouble held the banana up as high as he could reach, so that Jack could see it. And this time the monkey caught sight of the fruit.

With a chatter of delight at the good things he was getting to eat, Jack came down, but not exactly in the way Janet and Teddy wanted him to. For the pet *climbed* down the boxes, which were of different sizes, making many places where he could hold on by his hands and tail. He didn't jump at all!

With a chatter and a scramble, Jack reached the ground, ran around the net to where Trouble stood, and then just reached up, plucked the fruit from the little chap's hand and began to eat it. And it was all done so quickly that Ted and Janet hardly had time to say a word.

Finally, however, after laughing at the funny look on Trouble's face when he saw the monkey snatch away the banana, Teddy said:

"Oh, Jack! I didn't mean for you to come down that way! I wanted you to jump into the net! Here, you can't have the rest of that banana until you jump for it."

Teddy took the fruit away from his fuzzy pet, and Jack jabbered and chattered at the top of his voice, for he did not like this at all. To have a banana taken away when he was just half finished with it! That didn't seem fair!

"Come on! We'll try again, Jan," said Teddy, holding the half-eaten yellow fruit out of Jack's reach. For the monkey was jumping up trying to get back the banana.

"You'll have to get him up on top of the boxes again," Janet said.

"Yes, and I guess I'll have to break off a piece of this banana to get him to go up after it," her brother said. "Come on, Jack!" he cried.

Breaking what was left of the banana in half, Teddy once more climbed the step ladder and put the pulpy mass on top of the pile of boxes. Jack saw what was done, and in an instant he had climbed up.

"He's learning to go up fine!" declared Teddy, as he got down and moved the ladder away, so Jack would not use that in his descent. "If we can only make him jump now. Get ready, Trouble, to hold up the banana again."

"There isn't much left of it," Janet remarked.

"It's all there is until we go to the store for more," answered Teddy. "I guess it will do. We'll wait until he swallows what he's eating now, and then Trouble can hold up what is left."

Anxiously the Curlytops and their little brother watched Jack perched rather high on the tower of boxes. The monkey made short work of the small piece of banana that had been put on his high perch. Then he looked down for more.

"Hold it up, Trouble! Hold it up!" cried Teddy, at one end of the curtain net, while Janet held the other end.

"I hold it, but my hoots is gettin' tired," said the little fellow.

"Never mind, dear," consoled Janet. "If Jack doesn't jump this time we'll let you go. We can put a stick in the ground near the edge of the net, and tie the banana to that if Trouble is tired," she said to Teddy.

"Yes, but it won't be so good as Trouble, 'cause Jack likes him," Teddy answered. "Look out! I think he's going to jump!"

And that is just what Jack did!

With a chatter of delight as he saw Trouble holding up the piece of fruit, Jack stood for a moment on the edge of the pile of boxes, and then he leaped.

Straight down he jumped toward the lace curtain and toward Trouble, who held up the banana. But before the monkey landed there was a scream from the house, and Mrs. Martin came running out.

"Don't let Jack jump into my lace curtain! Don't do it, Curlytops!" exclaimed their mother. "He'll tear it to pieces. Stop him!"

But it was too late. Jack had jumped!

CHAPTER XVI

TOP IS GONE

Mrs. Martin ran as fast as she could from the back door of the house to that part of the yard where the Curlytops and Trouble were planning and practicing the new circus trick. Ted and Janet heard their mother's cry, and, for the first time, realized that perhaps they had done wrong in taking the lace curtain for a net.

And by the time Mrs. Martin reached the place where Trouble was standing, Jack had jumped into the curtain. Right into the middle of it he landed, and you can guess what happened.

Yes, Jack tore through, making a big hole in the lace. For it was not strong enough for even a play circus net, and, really, Ted and Janet should have known this.

Down through the hole in the curtain fell Jack, but he did not go quite all the way through. That is parts of the torn lace clung to him.

In another instant, after landing lightly on the ground, Jack sprang up, grabbed the banana away from Trouble, and then made a flying leap for the nearest tree, trailing the lace curtain after him, dragging it on the ground, catching it on the branches of the tree and tearing it worse than ever.

So suddenly did Jack snatch the piece of banana away from Baby William that the little fellow was knocked down, just as Jack, leaping away from the Italian hand-organ man, had knocked Teddy to the sidewalk.

"Oh! Oh!" wailed Trouble, and then he began to cry.

"Oh, Curlytops! Curlytops! What have you done?" exclaimed Mrs. Martin in dismay.

Teddy and Janet could not say a word. They seemed frightened and dazed when Jack, in his wild leap, pulled the curtain from their grasp.

"We—we—" began Janet.

"Didn't mean to," finished Teddy.

And then Jack began to chatter as he tried to tear loose the lace curtain which was tangled all about him as he sat perched in a tree, licking from his paws some bits of crushed banana.

With the crying of Trouble, the chatter of the monkey, and Mrs. Martin saying: "Oh dear! Oh dear!" again and again, there was quite a little excitement in the yard of the Curlytops just then.

"Poor Trouble!" sighed Janet, as she walked over to her little brother, who was crying and sitting on the ground where Jack had knocked him. "Did the monkey scratch you?"

But Trouble was sobbing too hard to answer.

"What in the world were you doing?" asked Mrs. Martin, as she picked Trouble up in her arms, and finally made him stop crying. "Why did you take one of my nice curtains?"

"We didn't know it was nice," Teddy answered. "And we had to get something for a net to have Jack jump in. I thought it was an old curtain."

"It wasn't one of my best ones," said his mother, "still I didn't want it torn. And it is of no use now. Look! All in shreds!"

Indeed that was the state of the curtain. For by this time Jack had managed to tear it off him, and it dangled in the tree like the tail of a broken kite.

"It will be good for dolls' dresses," said Janet. "And we can make other things to dress the animals up in for the circus."

"Oh, you Curlytops!" cried Mrs. Martin, trying not to laugh, for it was all rather funny in spite of the fact that one of her curtains was ruined. "However, it can't be helped," she went on. "Only, next time, come and ask me when you want a circus net."

"We will," promised Teddy. "But, anyhow, I guess we have taught Jack his new trick. He jumped like anything, and from the top of the tower, when he saw the banana."

"Oh, doesn't he look funny now!" cried Janet, pointing to the monkey, that was now sitting on a box and looking at the children and their mother. "He's got a lace frill on."

Part of the torn lace curtain was around Jack's neck, making him, indeed, look as though he wore a fancy collar.

"Him's got a bib on!" declared Trouble, now over his fright

Howard R. Garis

and crying spell, the first having caused the second. "Him's got a bib on 'ike Trouble when him eats bread and 'ilk."

"So he has, dear!" laughed Mrs. Martin. "And I guess Jack would rather be eating bread and milk than doing tricks in this pet show."

"Oh, no! He likes the circus! Or he will when we get it started," declared Teddy. "We've got lots to do yet, but I guess we can have it in about two weeks. We'll get Jack to practice his jump some more."

"Then we'll need more bananas—he ate the last one," remarked Janet. "And Mr. Nip likes them, too."

"We'll get more, but we won't make Jack do any more tricks to-day, Jan," decided Teddy. "Animals get cross if you keep 'em at their tricks too long."

"And I think I'll take Trouble into the house. He's had enough excitement for the day," said Mrs. Martin. "Don't take any more of my lace curtains," she added, as she moved toward the house.

"We won't," promised the Curlytops. Then they pulled from the tree, where Jack had torn his way out of it, the remainder of the lace curtain they had used for a landing net for the pet monkey.

It was two or three days after this, during which time the Curlytops had taught their pets several new little tricks, that their mother called Janet and Teddy to her one afternoon. Mrs. Martin held a letter in her hand, the postman having just left it for her.

"Here is something I want to talk to you children about," said their mother.

"Oh, is that a letter from Uncle Toby, and is he coming back to take his pets away before we've had the show?" asked Janet.

"No, indeed," answered her mother, with a laugh. "We haven't heard from Uncle Toby since he left for South America. I suppose, by this time, he is sitting in the jungle, watching hundreds of parrots and monkeys."

"I wish he'd send some more to us!" said Teddy.

"Oh, gracious sakes! I don't!" laughed Mrs. Martin. "I think we have quite enough as it is."

But of course the Curlytops did not think so.

"What I called you for," went on Mrs. Martin, "was to ask if you really intend to go on with this circus of yours. Do you really intend holding it?"

"Sure we do, Mother!" Teddy answered. "We're going to have a tent, and seats and everything."

"Are you going to charge money for persons to come in?"

"Yes," said Janet. "It's to be five cents for big boys and girls, and three cents for little ones like Trouble. Of course Trouble won't have to pay, 'cause he's going to be part of the show. But what is your letter about, Mother?"

"It's about your circus," was the answer. "At least now that I know you are really going on with the performance this letter will have something to do with it. This is a note from some ladies who, like me, belong to a charitable society," said

Mrs. Martin. "The secretary has just written me, asking if I can not think up some plan to raise money so some poor orphan children may be sent to the country to board for a few weeks this summer."

"Oh, can't we help the orphan children, as we helped the crippled children once?" asked Teddy.

"Just what I was going to say," went on his mother. "You may take in quite a few dollars giving your animal show, and I can think of no better way of spending it than to give it to the orphans. Besides, if it is known that the circus is for charity, many more people will come than would otherwise. So do you Curlytops want to help the orphans?"

"Of course!" said Janet.

"Sure!" cried Teddy.

"Me help, too! What is it?" asked Trouble, coming up just then.

"Oh, you're going to help all right!" laughed Janet. "You're going to drive Turnover and Skyrocket with my old rag doll, Miss Muffin, in the express wagon, and I'm sure you'll be so darling and funny that everyone will laugh."

"And I hope Jack does his jumping trick," said Teddy. "It would be great if we had Tip and Top to perform together. We could charge twenty-five cents for big people to come in if we had the two trick dogs."

"Well, one is better than none," said Janet. "It's a good thing we have Top."

"Yes," agreed Teddy, "I suppose it is. But I wonder where

Tip can be?"

But of course no one could tell him that.

So it was settled that the money that was taken in for the show of the Curlytops and their pets should go to the orphans, so they might have a few weeks in the green country during the hot summer.

The Curlytops were much excited that evening, telling their father about the performance for the orphans, and Mr. Martin agreed that no better use could be made of the money.

"You must take good care of your pets from now until the time of the show," he said. "Don't let them get away or become ill, or you will not be able to give a good circus."

"Let's go out to the barn now, and see if they are all right," proposed Janet.

"All right," agreed Teddy.

It was early evening, and light enough to see in the barn. Top and Skyrocket barked a welcome, Snuff and Turnover mewed their delight at seeing the children, and while Mr. Nip shrieked away about being a "crack-crack-cracker" Jack chattered. About the only quiet ones were the white rats and mice, and Slider, the alligator.

"They're all right, and ready for the circus," said Teddy as he came out and locked the door after him.

"Yes, I can hardly wait!" murmured Janet.

But in the morning there was bad news for the Curlytops. Their mother, who had gone out to the barn to open the door

160   Howard R. Garis

for the animals, came hurrying back to the house as Teddy and Janet descended for their breakfast.

"Where is Top?" asked Mrs. Martin.

"Top!" exclaimed Teddy. "Why, isn't he in the barn with Sky and the other pets?"

"No," answered his mother, shaking her head. "Top is gone! The barn door was locked, and all the other animals are there, but Top is gone!"

CHAPTER XVII

THE DOG SHOW

Teddy and Janet looked at each other in sorrow and dismay. It seemed that the worst had happened—Top missing just when they were getting ready for the show! First Tip was gone, and now Top! Could it be true?

"Are you sure, Mother?" asked Teddy. "Maybe Top is hiding behind a box or something."

"Let's go look!" proposed Janet.

"Oh, I'm sure he isn't there," said Mrs. Martin. "I called him, as I always do, when I go to let him and Skyrocket out. But Top did not come."

"Did Skyrocket?" asked Janet.

"Yes, he came rushing out of his kennel, barking and wagging his tail as if he would wag it off. And Snuff came out, and so did Turnover. But there was no Top."

Teddy started for the barn on the run, and so did Janet. Their mother followed more slowly. She felt very sorry for her Curlytops, as she knew they would be very sad over the loss of their second pet dog.

"The barn door is locked!" said Teddy, as he reached it and tried to go in.

"Yes, I locked it after me when I came out," his mother said. "I wanted to make sure that none of the other pets would get away. But the door was locked when I first went in this morning. It was locked just as you left it last night."

"Then I don't see how Top could have gotten out," Janet said.

"Unless there is some other place open in the barn—like a window," Mrs. Martin suggested.

"Let's look!" cried Teddy.

His mother turned the key in the padlock on the outside of the barn door. As the door opened and the Curlytops went in, they were greeted by barks of welcome from Skyrocket, by mews from Snuff and Turnover, the cats, by chattering from Mr. Jack, the monkey, and by shrill cries from Mr. Nip, the parrot, who called as loudly as he could:

"I'm a crack-crack-cracker!"

"They're all here but Top," said Mrs. Martin. And as the Curlytops looked around the barn they saw that this was so. Top was not in sight.

"Here, Top! Top! Top!" called Teddy, and he whistled. Mr. Nip also whistled, as loudly and clearly as the little boy himself. But there was no answer from his pet trick dog.

Janet ran over and looked in the box where Top always slept on a piece of carpet. The box was empty.

"Where do you s'pose he can be?" she asked her mother.

"That's what we must find out," was Mrs. Martin's answer. "We must look all through the barn. There are several places where he may have gotten out—or been taken out," she added a moment later.

It was Teddy who finally discovered the open window by which it was thought someone had entered the barn and taken Top out. The window was near the stalls used by the horses before Mr. Martin bought an automobile. In a corner, at the left of the stalls and too high from the floor of the barn for Top to have reached, even in his best jump, was a swinging window. This was open, as Teddy found, and when his mother and Janet came at his call, Mrs. Martin saw that the bolt had been broken.

"That is how it happened," she said. "Someone opened that window from the outside last night, crawled in, and took Top away. The dog himself could not have gotten out of that high window. Someone must have taken him."

"But wouldn't he bark and bite them?" asked Janet.

"Top was too friendly to bite anyone unless they harmed him," said her mother. "And I have no doubt but that this man—it must have been a man or a big boy—knew how to be nice to Top. Maybe they gave him a little piece of meat to chew on while they took him away."

"Oh dear!" sighed Janet. "How shall we ever get him back?"

"I'll call your father, and ask him what to do," remarked Mrs. Martin. "This is getting serious! Two of Uncle Toby's best pets gone! If he comes back he will think we did not take very good care of his animals."

"It wasn't our fault that a burglar came and took Top," said Teddy.

"No, dear," answered his mother. "But we must do what we can to get the dog back. I'll call your father."

Mr. Martin came quickly when he heard what had happened. He went to the barn to look, and he agreed with his wife that, during the night, someone had broken open the barn window, had crawled in, and had taken out Top.

"But why didn't they take Jack or Mr. Nip or Slider?" asked Teddy. "All our pets are nice. Why didn't they take more?"

"Maybe they didn't have time, or perhaps they were frightened away, or they may have wanted only Top," said Mr. Martin. "I think that last is the real reason. A trick poodle, like Top, is valuable. And if he could be placed in a show with his chum Tip, the two would earn a lot of money for whoever had them."

"Then," said Teddy, "we've got to find out who has Tip, and maybe then we'll get back Top."

"Yes," agreed his father, "but it isn't going to be easy. I'll report it to the police and also to the police of that town where Tip was taken."

"We can't have much of a show with Tip and Top gone," said Janet sadly.

"Well, not so very," answered Teddy, trying to make the best of it. "But if we don't get Top back we still have some pets left. The only thing is that Skyrocket has learned to do some tricks with Top, and if Top doesn't come back Sky can't do those tricks. Oh dear, I wish I knew who had our two trick poodles!"

"So do I!" chimed in Janet.

Mr. Martin called up the Cresco police and told them of the theft. Word was also sent to the town where the Curlytops had stopped for lunch the day they had brought home Uncle Toby's pets, when "Shorty" had been left on guard.

After that there was nothing to do but wait, though Ted and Jan wanted to go around among their friends, asking if, by chance, any of them had seen Top. And after breakfast their mother allowed them to do this.

To house after house of their friends and neighbors went the two Curlytops, telling the story of the theft of Top, and asking if anyone had seen him. But it was a hopeless search, as Mrs. Martin knew it would be. For whoever had taken Top, she felt sure, would hide him away, and not let him be seen in or about Cresco, where the pet animal was well known.

"What's the matter, Curlytops?" asked Policeman Cassidy, as he saw Teddy and Janet going along the street one day, having called at several houses, without getting any word about Top. "What's the matter? Can't you have the circus you were counting on?"

"We can't have it as nice as we want it with Top gone," answered Teddy, and then he explained about the theft, of which the policeman had not heard, having been away on his vacation.

"We've been looking all over for Top," added Janet, when her brother had finished, "but we can't find him."

Howard R. Garis

"You aren't looking in the right places," said the policeman. "You won't find him at the houses of any of your friends. If he was there he'd run back to you as soon as he got outside. Where you want to look is in some dog show."

"Dog show?" exclaimed Teddy.

"Yes," went on Mr. Cassidy. "I've heard about stolen dogs before. They are taken by men who want to make money. And since Top was a trick dog, as well as Tip, I'm sure someone has them who would put them in a show. So look for a dog show, and when you find it go in and look at the dogs. That's where you'll find Top, and maybe Tip, too. It's in a dog show you should be looking!"

"Yes," agreed Teddy, after thinking the matter over, "I guess we should. Thank you, Mr. Cassidy. Come on, Jan, we'll look for a dog show. Do you think there's one in Cresco, Mr. Cassidy?"

"None that I've heard of," the officer answered. "You'll see bill posters, and advertisements on the fences when there's a dog show around. Look for a dog show, and maybe you'll find your pets."

The Curlytops thanked him again, and walked off down the street together, filled with a new idea. Eagerly they scanned the walls and fences, seeking for some poster that would tell of a show. And it was not long before they saw just what they were looking for.

"See!" cried Janet, pointing to a red and black poster on a fence. "That tells of a show, Ted."

"Yes," agreed her brother, "so it does. But it's over in Canfield."

The advertisement told of "Professor Montelli's" wonderful collection of trained and trick dogs. A show would be given every afternoon and evening, the bill said, and, as Teddy had remarked, it was over in the neighboring town of Canfield.

"Maybe Tip would be there," suggested Janet, as she and her brother looked at the poster.

"And Top," added Ted.

"Let's go!" suddenly cried Janet. "I've got most of my allowance that daddy gave me. We can go on the trolley. It isn't far!"

Teddy thought it over for a moment. Then he made up his mind.

"All right!" he said. "Let's go to the dog show!"

CHAPTER XVIII

THE BLACK POODLES

Once they were in the trolley, going to Canfield, the two Curlytops felt quite happy. They were happy for one reason, because they were having a ride. Teddy and Janet always liked to be doing things and going somewhere, and this was one of those times.

And they were happy for another reason, because they felt sure they would find Top, and perhaps Tip. Who knew?

Policeman Cassidy had said the most likely place to find the missing poodles would be in a dog show. And they were going to a dog show.

"Do you s'pose mother will mind?" asked Janet of Ted, after they had ridden for a little way in the trolley.

"Oh, I don't guess so," he answered. "We'll soon be back, for it isn't very far to Canfield, and she said we could go out and hunt for Top."

"But maybe she didn't mean we were to go so far, and on a trolley."

"She didn't tell us *not* to!" declared Teddy.

"All right," went on Janet. "We're going, anyhow."

"Whereabout in Canfield do you—you Curlytops want to get out?" asked the trolley-car conductor.

"Oh, do you know us?" asked Janet, for the conductor had called the little boy and girl by the name so often given them.

"Well, I don't exactly know you," he answered. "But I would call you Curlytops if you were my children. For the tops of your heads are curly," he added with a laugh.

"Everybody calls us Curlytops," said Teddy. "And could you please let us out near the dog show?"

"The dog show," repeated the conductor, wonderingly.

"This one," went on Ted, taking from his pocket a hand bill of "Professor Montelli's Wondrous Aggregation of Canine Cut-ups." Teddy had found the bill in the street.

"Oh, that show!" exclaimed the conductor, with a laugh. "Why, that's only a little side-show in a tent near where this car runs. I'll let you get off there if you want to, but it isn't much of a show. It isn't a circus, you know," he said, as he started the car again, after a very fat lady had gotten off. "If you're looking for a circus this isn't it. The dog show is only a little side one—the kind they used to charge ten cents to go in and see after or before the regular circus. I hope you Curlytops aren't running away to see a circus," he added doubtfully.

"Oh, no, sir!" exclaimed Janet. "We're looking for our lost dog, and we thought maybe it was with this show. Two dogs we had, Tip and Top," she went on. "They were white poodles and they belonged to Uncle Toby and they could do tricks. But one was stolen when we were bringing them home, and the other night Top was taken from our barn. It's our dogs we're looking for, not a circus."

"Besides, we're going to have a circus of our own," added Teddy. "That is, we are if we get Tip and Top back."

"Do you think your dogs ran off to join a show?" the conductor asked.

"Oh, no!" answered Teddy. "They were taken away. But Mr. Cassidy—he's a policeman—said the right place to look for our dogs was in a dog show, so we're looking."

"Well, this Professor Montelli, as he calls himself, has a dog show near the end of my trolley line," said the conductor. "I don't know much about it, as it only came there yesterday. It's in a little tent—a regular side show. I'll put you off near it. But do you think it will be safe for you to go there alone and ask for your lost dogs?"

"Oh, we won't go right in and ask for them," explained Teddy. He and his sister had talked it over, and they had made up their minds what they would do. "We'll just go into the show—'cause we have money to pay for our tickets," the Curlytop boy explained. "Then if we see Tip and Top there we'll take 'em right away."

"That's what we will!" declared Janet. "And if that show man won't give our dogs to us we'll call a policeman."

"Well, I guess you Curlytops can take care of yourselves," laughed the conductor. "You get off three blocks from here, and then you'll be right near the dog show. Good luck to you!"

"Thank you," replied Teddy and Janet.

They saw the tent—a small one with a few flags on it—almost as soon as they alighted from the trolley car. It was about three o'clock, and a crowd about the tent showed that the performance was going on, or would soon start.

Professor Montelli's name was painted on a strip of canvas over the entrance to the tent, and on either side were painted pictures of dogs doing all sorts of queer tricks. One picture was that of a dog jumping off a high platform into a tank of water.

"Oh, if we could only make our monkey Jack do a trick like that!" whispered Janet to Teddy.

"Maybe we can," he whispered back, as they walked up to the tent. "But monkeys don't like water, I guess. We might get Skyrocket to do the jump. We'll try. But now let's see if Tip or Top are here in this show."

A man standing in a booth outside the tent was calling out in a loud voice:

"Step right up, ladies and gentlemen! Step right up, boys and girls! The big show is about to begin!"

He ruffled a bundle of red tickets in his hand and went on:

"Pay your dime and step right up. You'll see the world-famed aggregation of canine cut-ups! The funniest dogs you ever saw doing the funniest tricks! There are hound dogs, bulldogs, setter dogs, fox terriers, big dogs, little dogs, all good dogs, and some poodle dogs!"

Ted and Janet looked at each other.

"Poodles!" whispered the Curlytops.

Tip and Top were white poodles!

"Come on! Let's go in!" said Teddy boldly.

He stepped up to the booth, bought two tickets, and he and Janet went into the tent. At one end was a raised platform, hung about with red cloth. On the platform were some chairs, a table, some pedestals, some paper-covered hoops and other things used in the dog tricks. There were also some board benches, like circus seats, in the tent.

"Come on up front, where we can see the dogs better," said Ted to his sister. "If we see Tip or Top we'll call them right down to us off the platform."

There were as yet not many persons in the tent, and the Curlytops had no trouble getting front seats. Then they anxiously waited for the performance to begin, which it did in a little while.

Out on the platform came a man with a very black moustache and a little whip. The moustache was under his nose and the whip in his hands. He looked around at the audience, and then in a sing-song voice said:

"Ladies an' gen'men: With your kind attention an' permission I will now show you what my dogs can do. Let 'em on, Jack," he called to someone back of the platform.

A moment later about ten dogs rushed up on the platform, barking and wagging their tails. Every one of the dogs looked anxiously at the black-eyed and black-moustached man, as if afraid he would hit them with the whip he carried. Each dog seemed to know his or her place, and went to chair, box, or platform, until all were arranged in a half circle back of the man.

"First Lulu, the highest jumper in the world, will perform some tricks," said Professor Montelli. "Here, Lulu," he called, and a long, thin greyhound leaped from a chair and stood ready. This dog jumped over a pile of high baskets, and through some of them, there being no bottoms to them. Then the greyhound leaped over a high pile of chairs.

In turn the other dogs did tricks, some of which the Curlytops had seen before, and some of which were new. They quite enjoyed the show, or they would have done so had they not been worrying about getting their own dogs back. They looked anxiously at the dogs on the platform. None of them was Tip or Top.

I shall not tell you all about the tricks the dogs in this show did, for I want to tell you about the circus the Curlytops had. Enough to say that Professor Montelli seemed to know a great deal about dogs, though I can not say the trick animals loved him. They seemed more afraid than anything else.

"Well, I guess we shan't find Tip or Top here," said Ted to Janet after a while. "There aren't any white poodles like ours."

"No, I guess not," sadly agreed the little girl.

But just then Professor Montelli stepped to the edge of the platform and said:

"This ends our regular performance, ladies an' gen'men, but I have two more dogs to show you. I have not finished training them yet, an' they can do only a few tricks, but I want you to be satisfied, an' think that you got your money's worth, so you will recommend my show to your friends. I will now show you two more trick dogs. Bring on the poodles, Jack," he called to his assistant.

Ted and Janet looked at each other, quickly.

"Poodles!" they murmured, but they did not speak out loud.

The same thought was in each of their minds. If the poodles should be Tip and Top!

A barking was heard back of the platform, and, a moment later, on rushed two dogs, exactly the same kind of poodles as were Tip and Top, and exactly the same size.

But alas! Tip and Top were white, while these poodles were jet black!

CHAPTER XIX

A HAPPY REUNION

The hearts of the Curlytops had beaten high with hope when they heard Professor Montelli speak of some poodles. But when they saw that the two dogs were black, instead of white, their hearts sank.

"They look just like Tip and Top, but of course they can't be," whispered Janet, as the showman began clearing the stage platform in readiness for the poodles to do some tricks.

"No," answered Ted, in disappointed tones, "Tip and Top were white—not black, except for little spots. These dogs are black all over. We might as well go home. Maybe Policeman Cassidy knows of another dog show."

"Oh, let's stay and see just one poodle trick," begged Janet.

"All right," agreed Teddy.

So the Curlytops remained in their seats, with the others of the audience. The two black poodles barked, wagged their tails, and looked at Professor Montelli.

"Come on now, King! Turn a somersault!" suddenly cried

the dark-moustached man. Instantly one of the black poodles —the one called "King," began turning somersault after somersault. Right out to the end of the platform he turned them, and then he stood there, wagging his tail and waiting for the applause, which he seemed to expect.

And the people did clap. They liked the poodle's trick. Janet leaned over and whispered to Teddy:

"That's just the same trick Tip did!"

"Yes," agreed the Curlytop boy. "But it can't be Tip."

"No, I s'pose not," sighed Janet.

"Come back here, King," suddenly called the trainer. "Now, Emperor," he went on, pointing his whip at the other poodle. "It is your turn. Walk on your hind legs!"

The other dog did not seem to understand. It slunk away and growled a little.

"Here! None of that!" cried the trainer. "You must do as I say! Walk on your hind legs!"

Still the dog would not mind.

"Emperor is not so good a dog as King," said the man, apologizing to the audience. "I have not had him so long, and he does not do his tricks very well. But I will make him!"

Suddenly he flicked the dog he called "Emperor" with the whip!

The dog let out a howl of pain.

"Here! Stop that!" cried Teddy, almost before he knew what he was saying.

"Yes, don't hurt the dogs," added a lady, looking kindly at the Curlytops. "The little boy is right."

"I did not mean to hurt him," explained Professor Montelli, smiling, but his smile was not a kind one. He seemed to be a cruel man, but he seemed to know that he must not be cruel to his dogs in public. "Come, Emperor!" he called more gently. "Walk on your hind legs!"

This time the black poodle did so, walking around the stage. Again Janet leaned over and whispered to her brother:

"Top used to do that same trick!"

"Yes," agreed Teddy. "That's right."

And then a strange thing happened. All at once the two poodles put their noses together, as though talking, which they may have been doing in dog language. And then the one the man had called Emperor suddenly jumped on top of the back of the dog called King, and King began walking around the stage, giving the other a ride!

The people clapped at this trick, and the two Curlytops grew strangely excited. Ted and Janet looked at each other, standing up in their seats.

"Ted, do you know what I think?" said his sister. "I think those two dogs are really Tip and Top—our poodles! That's exactly the same trick they did in Uncle Toby's house."

"But how could they be Tip and Top when they're black, and Tip and Top were white?" asked Teddy.

"I don't know," Janet answered. "But I'm sure they are our dogs. Maybe they've been in the coal bin and got all black. And, oh, Ted! Look!"

Something else happening on the platform of the dog show tent. The black poodle called King began walking around in a little circle in the middle of the stage. And, while thus moving, the other poodle began to jump over its companion's back. First this way and then that one poodle jumped over the other poodle's back.

"Why! Why!" cried Teddy. "That's the other trick we saw them do, Janet! That's the trick Mrs. Watson said Uncle Toby taught them—I mean taught Tip and Top."

"Yes," agreed Janet. "And I know these dogs are our poodles—I don't care if they are black!" Then, before Ted could stop her, she called: "Here, Tip! Here, Top! Come on!"

Instantly the two black poodles jumped down off the stage, and with barks of joy, and mad waggings of their little tails, ran to the Curlytops.

"Oh, Top!" cried Janet, as she patted his head, "I'm so glad we found you! I'd know you anywhere, even if you are black!"

Both dogs knew the children, though of course Top, having been with them longer, knew them best. Tip had been taken away soon after being removed from Uncle Toby's house, but when Tip saw that Top was friendly with the children, Tip was joyful also.

I call the black dogs Tip and Top, for they were really the missing poodles, and I will explain how it was their color was changed.

No sooner did Ted and Janet call the black poodles to them than Professor Montelli grew very angry indeed. He jumped down off the platform, and, going to where the Curlytops stood at their seats, with the dogs frisking around them, the trainer cried:

"Here! What do you mean by calling my dogs away when I am making them do tricks? What do you children mean?"

"These aren't your dogs—they're *ours*!" declared Ted.

"Yours! Nonsense!" blustered the trainer. "These are my dogs. I have had them a long while!"

"Not both of them!" said Janet, who remembered what the man had said. "You told us you hadn't had Emperor very long."

"Well, I have the other! They are both my dogs!" cried the angry man. "If you have lost any dogs you had better look somewhere for them. Get out of my tent and give me back the poodles!"

He made a move to thrust Ted and Janet to one side and pick up the poodles, but a man in the audience said:

"Not so fast, Professor. It seems to me that by the way these dogs came to this girl and boy when called that there may be something in their claim. Did you lose two dogs?" he asked Ted and Janet.

"Yes, sir," they answered. And then Ted told how Tip was taken out of their automobile some weeks before, while Top was stolen from their barn a night or two previous.

"Nonsense! As if I had their dogs!" sneered the trainer.

"What kind of poodles did you lose, as you say?" he asked.

"Just exactly the same kind as these, and they did the same tricks," Ted answered. "We can make these do the same tricks you did, and some more, too," he added.

"I don't believe it!" growled the trainer.

"Let's show 'em, Ted!" cried Janet.

And then and there, down on the ground in the tent, while the crowd looked on, the Curlytops put the two black poodles through the tricks Tip and Top used to do.

"It begins to look as though there was something in their claim," said the man who had acted as the friend of Ted and Janet.

"Those are my dogs!" declared the Professor, getting more and more angry. "Tell me—what color were the poodles you had?" he asked Janet and Ted.

"Well," Ted answered slowly, "Tip and Top were white, except Tip had a little black spot on the end of his tail, and Top had a black spot on his head—on the top."

"There! What did I tell you?" cried the Professor. "Their poodles were *white* and mine are *black*! They can't be the same! Here, King and Emperor!" he cried, and, stooping down he made a grab for the little dogs that were staying near Ted and Janet.

With barks and growls the poodles sprang away from the angry man. And, as it happened, the one the man had called "King" ran against a pail of water that was near the bottom of the platform. The pail was upset and some of the water splashed over the black dog.

Then a queer change took place. Instead of being pure black, the poodle became streaked black and white! The black color began running out of its hair, and formed a little inky pool on the ground beneath the animal.

"Look! Look!" cried Janet, pointing.

"Those dogs were *colored* black—they're white poodles dyed black!" cried the man who had taken the part of the Curlytops. "Now what have you to say?" he asked the animal trainer.

"Well—er—those dogs are mine! I don't know who stained 'em black. But I bought 'em of a young man—"

"Was his name Shorty?" asked Ted.

"Well, maybe it was," admitted the showman. "What has that got to do with it? Those are my dogs!"

"They're ours!" insisted Ted. "Shorty was watching our auto when Tip was stolen," he went on, "and he knew where we were taking Top. I guess Shorty broke into our barn the other night, and took Top and colored him black. These are our poodles, and we're going to have them!"

"It looks as though they had you, Professor," said the kind man.

"And we're going to get a policeman!" added Janet.

"Oh, well, if you're sure they are your dogs, take 'em!" growled the showman. "I didn't know they were stolen. A young fellow sold me one some time ago, and I bought the other of him day before yesterday. I did color the dogs black," he admitted, "because they don't get so dirty as white ones. The dye will wash off," he said. "If you are sure these are your poodles, take 'em along!" he said to Ted and Janet.

"Oh, we're sure all right!" cried Janet. And then she took Top up in her arms, while Teddy carried the partly black and partly white Tip out of the tent, while the audience laughed and some clapped.

"The show's over!" growled the black-moustached man. "And if I get hold of that Shorty I'll have him arrested for selling me stolen dogs. They were valuable, too—as good trick dogs as I ever saw. Do you want to sell them to me?" he asked the Curlytops.

"No, sir!" cried Teddy and Janet as they hurried out of the tent. "We're going to have a circus of our own with 'em!"

And, happy and joyful, with the delighted Tip and Top in their arms, the Curlytops started for home.

CHAPTER XX

THE CURLYTOPS' CIRCUS

Hurrying along, as if afraid that Professor Montelli might run after them and take Tip and Top away again, Teddy and Janet went to the corner where they had left the trolley car. Some boys and girls who had been in the dog show followed the Curlytops, and men and women smiled at the children.

"Here comes a car!" cried Ted, as he saw one approaching. "Have we got enough money left to take us home, Jan?" he asked, for his sister had the cash.

"I guess so," she answered. "If we haven't we'll ask the conductor please to charge it."

The car stopped and with Janet holding Top and Ted with Tip in his arms, the children got aboard.

"Well, I see you got your dogs back," came a voice, and, looking up, the Curlytops saw the same conductor they had ridden out with from Cresco.

"I didn't think I'd have you back with me so soon," he said. "But I'm glad to see you. It's sort of against the rules to bring dogs on trolley cars, but I guess yours will be all right, as long as they're trick circus dogs."

"Shall we make 'em do some tricks for you?" asked Teddy, as he and his sister took their seats.

"Well, not now, thank you," the conductor answered, with a smile as the car started off, leaving behind the curious crowd. "I'll soon be so busy collecting fares that I won't have time to watch."

"Then we'll send you a ticket to our circus," promised Janet, "'cause you were so kind to us."

"Thank you," replied the conductor. "I shall be glad to come. You can take my name and mail the ticket to me at the car house. I like animals," and he patted the heads of Tip and Top. "But what makes one black, and the other streaked black and white?" he asked.

"They're colored, but it will wash off," answered Ted. "The Professor, or maybe Shorty, dyed our white poodles black."

You can imagine how surprised Mr. and Mrs. Martin were when Ted and Janet came in with the lost dogs—one black and the other white and black.

"I was just going to telephone to the police and have them start to look for you!" cried their mother. "I was worried. Where have you been?"

"To a dog show, where we found Tip and Top," said Janet.

Then they told the whole story, and Mr. and Mrs. Martin were much surprised at what the Curlytops had done.

"As it was, you did just the right thing," said their father.

"Though I wouldn't like to have you do it again. However, I'm glad you have your pets back, though Tip isn't exactly a beauty."

"They'll be all right after they have had a bath," said Janet.

And the poodles were, coming from the tub as white as snow. Later it was learned that the young man known as Shorty had not really taken Tip from the automobile. But he had gotten a chum of his to do it, and afterward the two had sold the dog. They sold him to Professor Montelli, who used to have a side show with a circus, but who, after a quarrel, started out for himself, traveling around the country giving exhibitions.

Shorty, having heard the talk of the Martin family while he was acting as guard of the automobile load of pets, knew where Top was being taken, to Cresco. And it was he who broke into the barn and took away the poodle. For, as I have told you, while one dog was valuable for the tricks he could do, the two, doing tricks together, were worth much more.

Professor Montelli may not have known the poodles were stolen, and he may, as he said, have dyed them with harmless black color to keep their white coats from getting dirty. But the police said they thought the dog trainer had a hand, with Shorty, in the thefts, and this may have been so. At any rate the Curlytops had their pet poodles back, and they heard nothing more of Shorty or the showman.

"And now we can give our circus!" cried Janet one afternoon, when she and Teddy, with Trouble, were feeding their pets in the barn.

It did not take long to make arrangements for the show. Jimmy Norton's father secured a large tent for the Curlytops and their friends, and the tent was set up in a lot not far from the Martin house. Several boys and girls helped make the arrangements, and Mr. Martin sent up from the store a pile of boxes and boards which some of his men made into seats.

Mrs. Martin told the ladies who had asked her to help raise money for the orphans that the Curlytops were going to give all they took in at the circus to help the poor children. And when this became known many grown folk, as well as boys and girls, bought tickets for the performance.

It was to be given one afternoon, and you can imagine all the work that had to be done to get ready. But some of the fathers and mothers of the chums of the Curlytops helped, leaving to Ted and Janet the work of getting the animals ready to do their tricks. Jack Turton was to be a fat little clown, riding on a pony his father had bought for him. Harry Kent and some other boys were to help Teddy, and some of Jan's girl friends offered to help her.

And we must not forget Trouble. As arranged, he was to come into the tent at a certain time, driving Skyrocket, the dog, and Turnover, the cat, hitched to his little express wagon, with funny Miss Muffin on the seat.

At last the day of the circus came. Into the tent were moved the cages of the white mice and the white rats, the tank containing Slider, the pet alligator, the cage of Mr. Nip, the parrot, and the box of Jack, the monkey. Snuff, Skyrocket and Turnover were on hand. Tip and Top were all ready to perform their tricks.

"Do you think we'll have a big crowd?" asked Janet of Ted, when everything was arranged and it was almost time for the show to begin.

"Sure we will!" he answered. "Everybody I met is coming—all the fellows and girls and a lot of men and women. We'll make a lot of money for the orphans."

"I wish Uncle Toby could be here to see it all," went on Janet, as she took a last look inside the tent to make sure everything was in order "He'd be surprised at some of the things his pets can do."

"Yes, I wish Uncle Toby could be here," said her brother. "It's queer about him. He never answered any of daddy's letters. South America must be a good way off, for Uncle Toby hasn't gotten there yet."

"Well," began Ted. "I guess—" and then Harry Kent called:

"Hey, Ted! You'd better look at Slider! He's trying to crawl out of his tank."

"It isn't time for him to start his act yet!" answered the Curlytop boy. "I'll have to give him a bit of meat to quiet him!"

And a little while after that the audience began to enter the tent. Boys and girls, of course, were the first, but there were a number of men and women, too, and it was not long before every seat was taken. Mr. and Mrs. Martin just had to be there—they couldn't stay away when the Curlytops were giving a show. Besides, Mother Martin had to help Trouble dress for his act.

"Oh, we're going to have a big crowd!" said Janet excitedly to Teddy, in the little dressing room behind the stage. There was a stage almost like the one Professor Montelli had in his dog show.

"You better go out and make your talk now," went on Janet to her brother. "The tent won't hold many more, and we want to start."

"All right," agreed Teddy. It had been decided that he was to make a little speech of welcome. Soon he was out in front, bowing as he did when he "spoke a piece" in school.

"Ladies and gentlemen," began Teddy, "and boys and girls. We're glad you came to our circus, and we hope you will like our pets and what they do. And my little brother, Trouble, is going to do an act by himself. He—"

"Here I is!" suddenly cried Trouble, coming out behind Teddy. "I do my act now!"

"No! No!" said Teddy, while the audience laughed. For Trouble was only half dressed, having rushed out of the room back of the stage when he heard his name mentioned.

"Here, William! Come back and let me finish!" said his mother, and she reached out her hand and pulled Trouble back to her.

"Now the show will start," Teddy finished, amid laughter.

The first act was a tableau with Ted, Janet and their boy and girl helpers, not forgetting Trouble, of course, posing on the stage with their pets. Gathered about the children were the dogs, the cats, Mr. Nip, the parrot, Jack the monkey, the white mice and the white rats in cages, and Slider, the pet alligator. Down in the audience Harry Weldon played the mouth organ. He was the "orchestra."

No sooner had Harry started to play than Tip, Top and Skyrocket barked, the cats mewed, the monkey chattered and

Mr. Nip cried:

"I'm a crack-crack-cracker!"

You should have heard the audience clap then!

One after another the animals did their tricks, Ted, Janet and the other boys and girls helping. Mr. Nip, the parrot, after he had been quieted down, walked up and down a little ladder, that was balanced like a see-saw over a tiny board. Mr. Nip would walk to one end of the ladder, and it would go down with him. Then he would walk to the other end, which would then sway downward. And when he had finished this trick Mr. Nip cried:

"Help! Fire! Police!" and flew over on Janet's shoulder.

"He's as good as a watch dog, that parrot is," said Policeman Cassidy, who had come to the show, as had also the kind trolley car conductor. "He's a regular burglar alarm, he is!"

Snuff and Turnover did their tricks, some separately and some together. One of the tricks they did together was to run and jump through a paper hoop, and when Turnover had landed on the other side, through the hoop, he lay down and rolled over and over—one of the first tricks the Curlytops had taught their pet.

Again the audience clapped and laughed. But there was more to come. Tip and Top did the tricks for which they were famous, separately and together, one dog walking on his hind legs, and the other turning somersaults. Then one dog got on the other's back, the two going around the stage together. And as a climax they did the trick by which Ted and Janet had recognized their pets in Professor Montelli's tent, one dog leaping over the other's back, while moving along.

"Now, Jan, you do your trick with the white mice and the alligator while Harry Kent and I fix up the tower for Jack to jump from," said Ted. "And Jack can do his clown tricks, too."

It had been decided that while Teddy and his helper were putting in place the tower for the monkey to leap from something must be done to amuse the audience.

So Janet had said she would do some little tricks with the mice, rats, and alligator, while Harry, the fat little boy clown, would turn somersaults and handsprings on the stage.

This went off very well. Janet fixed the slanting board for Slider to coast "down hill," and when the alligator had done this the audience laughed its hardest. Then some of the rats and mice did simple tricks, two of the larger rats pulling a little toy wagon in which rode two mice.

However, these pets did not do as well as the others, for the two in the wagon kept jumping out and Janet had to keep putting them back.

Jack, the fat little clown, made a big "hit." He was really very funny, and when, toward the end of his act, he got too near the edge of the stage and fell into the lap of big Oscar North, the audience thought it was all part of the show, and not an accident, and clapped most loudly. However, Jack was not hurt, and only laughed at the mishap.

By this time the tower was ready. It reached nearly to the top of the tent, and as the boxes had been covered with green branches they made a nice appearance.

"Up, Jack! Up!" called Ted, climbing up the stepladder and placing the banana on top of the tower. Then Ted had to hurry the ladder away, after Jack had climbed up to the top, for fear the monkey would climb down that same way instead of jumping as he was wanted to do.

Ted and Harry Kent held the net at the foot of the tower. This time the net was not a lace curtain, but some old bags sewed together. Janet held up the bit of banana, and, after he had eaten the piece on top of his perch, the monkey looked down at the other bit of fruit.

"Come on, Jack! Jump!" cried Teddy.

And to the delight of the Curlytops, Jack jumped his very best, landing in the net and bouncing up and down.

"Good trick! Good trick!" cried the trolley car conductor, clapping the loudest of all.

After that Jack did a number of other simple tricks, and then it was time for Trouble to come on in his act. Only a few knew what the little fellow was to do. But when the curtains on the stage were pulled apart by Mrs. Martin and the little fellow walked out, dressed like the pictures of Cupid on valentines, driving the dog and cat harnessed to the wagon, with queer Miss Muffin on the seat, you should have heard the people laugh and clap!

"Didap! Didap!" cried Trouble to his dog and cat team. "Didap an' go fast!"

Around the stage went Skyrocket and Turnover, behaving very nicely; and when he had made one round Trouble stood in the middle of the stage and made a low bow, as his mother had taught him to do.

"He's a cute little chap!" said Policeman Cassidy.

Howard R. Garis

And then came the last scene of all, where Ted, Janet, Trouble and their boy and girl helpers, with all the pets, except the parrot, alligator and rats and mice, marched around the stage, while the mouth organ was loudly played.

"That's the end of the show! Much obliged to you all for coming!" called out Teddy.

"And let's see how much we made for the orphans!" exclaimed Janet, before any of the audience had a chance to leave.

There was a laugh at this.

"You did very well, Curlytops, and Trouble also," said Mrs. Martin, as the children began to take off their costumes, for they had all dressed especially for the occasion.

"I never thought the pets would act so well," added Mr. Martin.

"And did we make much money?" Janet wanted to know.

Mr. Martin was counting it. As he dropped the last penny back into the cash box he announced:

"It is ninety-nine dollars and one cent."

"Well, here's ninety-nine cents to make it an even hundred dollars!" cried a jolly voice at the tent entrance, and in walked a man who seemed to be a stranger. But at the second look Mr. Martin cried:

"Uncle Toby!"

"Yes, Uncle Toby!" laughed the man. "I got here a little too late for the show, but you can give it over again for me, and I'll put as much again in the collection box as you have there. How are all my pets?" and he laughed again and looked at the Curlytops as well as at the animals.

"We're well, thank you," said Janet, shyly.

"And Tip and Top were taken away but we got them back," added Ted.

"An' Mr. Nip he catch a bu'glar!" lisped Trouble.

"My! My! There must have been a lot of excitement while I have been gone!" laughed Uncle Toby, for it was, indeed, he.

"When did you get back from South America?" asked Mr. Martin.

"I didn't go," answered Uncle Toby. "I got all ready to go, but changed my mind and went to Canada instead. I'm going back to live in my old house."

"And will you—will you take your pets?" asked Teddy.

"Well, not right away," answered Uncle Toby. "You may keep them as long as you like. I wish I had been here for the show, but here's the ninety-nine cents I promised, and if you give the show for me later on I'll give a hundred dollars for the orphans."

"Oh, how lovely!" cried Janet. "Let's start and give it now!"

It was, however, a little too late in the day for that. But, a week later, Uncle Toby did see all the pets put through their tricks and he gave another hundred to the orphan fund, so that many of the poor children had a fine vacation time in the country.

"Well, we certainly had a lot of fun with all the animals," said Janet one day, when she and Teddy were playing out under the trees with the dogs and the cats.

"Yes," he agreed, "we did. We had as much fun this summer as if we had gone away. And I wonder what we can do next?"

"Oh, something, I guess," said Janet. "What I'm going to do now is go in and get something to eat."

"I'm a crack-crack-cracker!" shrieked Mr. Nip from his perch.

"Well, I want something more than crackers!" laughed Janet.

"So do I!" agreed Teddy. "We'll get some bread and jam and also feed our pets. I guess they're hungry, too."

And while the Curlytops are thus engaged we will say good-bye to Janet, Teddy and Trouble.

THE END

Choose from Thousands of 1stWorldLibrary Classics By

A. M. Barnard	Booth Tarkington	Edward Everett Hale
Ada Leverson	Boyd Cable	Edward J. O'Biren
Adolphus William Ward	Bram Stoker	Edward S. Ellis
Aesop	C. Collodi	Edwin L. Arnold
Agatha Christie	C. E. Orr	Eleanor Atkins
Alexander Aaronsohn	C. M. Ingleby	Eleanor Hallowell Abbott
Alexander Kielland	Carolyn Wells	Eliot Gregory
Alexandre Dumas	Catherine Parr Traill	Elizabeth Gaskell
Alfred Gatty	Charles A. Eastman	Elizabeth McCracken
Alfred Ollivant	Charles Amory Beach	Elizabeth Von Arnim
Alice Duer Miller	Charles Dickens	Ellem Key
Alice Turner Curtis	Charles Dudley Warner	Emerson Hough
Alice Dunbar	Charles Farrar Browne	Emilie F. Carlen
Allen Chapman	Charles Ives	Emily Bronte
Alleyne Ireland	Charles Kingsley	Emily Dickinson
Ambrose Bierce	Charles Klein	Enid Bagnold
Amelia E. Barr	Charles Hanson Towne	Enilor Macartney Lane
Amory H. Bradford	Charles Lathrop Pack	Erasmus W. Jones
Andrew Lang	Charles Romyn Dake	Ernie Howard Pie
Andrew McFarland Davis	Charles Whibley	Ethel May Dell
Andy Adams	Charles Willing Beale	Ethel Turner
Angela Brazil	Charlotte M. Braeme	Ethel Watts Mumford
Anna Alice Chapin	Charlotte M. Yonge	Eugene Sue
Anna Sewell	Charlotte Perkins Stetson	Eugenie Foa
Annie Besant	Clair W. Hayes	Eugene Wood
Annie Hamilton Donnell	Clarence Day Jr.	Eustace Hale Ball
Annie Payson Call	Clarence E. Mulford	Evelyn Everett-green
Annie Roe Carr	Clemence Housman	Everard Cotes
Annonaymous	Confucius	F. H. Cheley
Anton Chekhov	Coningsby Dawson	F. J. Cross
Archibald Lee Fletcher	Cornelis DeWitt Wilcox	F. Marion Crawford
Arnold Bennett	Cyril Burleigh	Fannie E. Newberry
Arthur C. Benson	D. H. Lawrence	Federick Austin Ogg
Arthur Conan Doyle	Daniel Defoe	Ferdinand Ossendowski
Arthur M. Winfield	David Garnett	Fergus Hume
Arthur Ransome	Dinah Craik	Florence A. Kilpatrick
Arthur Schnitzler	Don Carlos Janes	Fremont B. Deering
Arthur Train	Donald Keyhoe	Francis Bacon
Atticus	Dorothy Kilner	Francis Darwin
B.H. Baden-Powell	Dougan Clark	Frances Hodgson Burnett
B. M. Bower	Douglas Fairbanks	Frances Parkinson Keyes
B. C. Chatterjee	E. Nesbit	Frank Gee Patchin
Baroness Emmuska Orczy	E. P. Roe	Frank Harris
Baroness Orczy	E. Phillips Oppenheim	Frank Jewett Mather
Basil King	E. S. Brooks	Frank L. Packard
Bayard Taylor	Earl Barnes	Frank V. Webster
Ben Macomber	Edgar Rice Burroughs	Frederic Stewart Isham
Bertha Muzzy Bower	Edith Van Dyne	Frederick Trevor Hill
Bjornstjerne Bjornson	Edith Wharton	Frederick Winslow Taylor

Friedrich Kerst
Friedrich Nietzsche
Fyodor Dostoyevsky
G.A. Henty
G.K. Chesterton
Gabrielle E. Jackson
Garrett P. Serviss
Gaston Leroux
George A. Warren
George Ade
Geroge Bernard Shaw
George Cary Eggleston
George Durston
George Ebers
George Eliot
George Gissing
George MacDonald
George Meredith
George Orwell
George Sylvester Viereck
George Tucker
George W. Cable
George Wharton James
Gertrude Atherton
Gordon Casserly
Grace E. King
Grace Gallatin
Grace Greenwood
Grant Allen
Guillermo A. Sherwell
Gulielma Zollinger
Gustav Flaubert
H. A. Cody
H. B. Irving
H.C. Bailey
H. G. Wells
H. H. Munro
H. Irving Hancock
H. R. Naylor
H. Rider Haggard
H. W. C. Davis
Haldeman Julius
Hall Caine
Hamilton Wright Mabie
Hans Christian Andersen
Harold Avery
Harold McGrath
Harriet Beecher Stowe
Harry Castlemon
Harry Coghill
Harry Houidini

Hayden Carruth
Helent Hunt Jackson
Helen Nicolay
Hendrik Conscience
Hendy David Thoreau
Henri Barbusse
Henrik Ibsen
Henry Adams
Henry Ford
Henry Frost
Henry James
Henry Jones Ford
Henry Seton Merriman
Henry W Longfellow
Herbert A. Giles
Herbert Carter
Herbert N. Casson
Herman Hesse
Hildegard G. Frey
Homer
Honore De Balzac
Horace B. Day
Horace Walpole
Horatio Alger Jr.
Howard Pyle
Howard R. Garis
Hugh Lofting
Hugh Walpole
Humphry Ward
Ian Maclaren
Inez Haynes Gillmore
Irving Bacheller
Isabel Cecilia Williams
Isabel Hornibrook
Israel Abrahams
Ivan Turgenev
J.G.Austin
J. Henri Fabre
J. M. Barrie
J. M. Walsh
J. Macdonald Oxley
J. R. Miller
J. S. Fletcher
J. S. Knowles
J. Storer Clouston
J. W. Duffield
Jack London
Jacob Abbott
James Allen
James Andrews
James Baldwin

James Branch Cabell
James DeMille
James Joyce
James Lane Allen
James Lane Allen
James Oliver Curwood
James Oppenheim
James Otis
James R. Driscoll
Jane Abbott
Jane Austen
Jane L. Stewart
Janet Aldridge
Jens Peter Jacobsen
Jerome K. Jerome
Jessie Graham Flower
John Buchan
John Burroughs
John Cournos
John F. Kennedy
John Gay
John Glasworthy
John Habberton
John Joy Bell
John Kendrick Bangs
John Milton
John Philip Sousa
John Taintor Foote
Jonas Lauritz Idemil Lie
Jonathan Swift
Joseph A. Altsheler
Joseph Carey
Joseph Conrad
Joseph E. Badger Jr
Joseph Hergesheimer
Joseph Jacobs
Jules Vernes
Julian Hawthrone
Julie A Lippmann
Justin Huntly McCarthy
Kakuzo Okakura
Karle Wilson Baker
Kate Chopin
Kenneth Grahame
Kenneth McGaffey
Kate Langley Bosher
Kate Langley Bosher
Katherine Cecil Thurston
Katherine Stokes
L. A. Abbot
L. T. Meade

L. Frank Baum
Latta Griswold
Laura Dent Crane
Laura Lee Hope
Laurence Housman
Lawrence Beasley
Leo Tolstoy
Leonid Andreyev
Lewis Carroll
Lewis Sperry Chafer
Lilian Bell
Lloyd Osbourne
Louis Hughes
Louis Joseph Vance
Louis Tracy
Louisa May Alcott
Lucy Fitch Perkins
Lucy Maud Montgomery
Luther Benson
Lydia Miller Middleton
Lyndon Orr
M. Corvus
M. H. Adams
Margaret E. Sangster
Margret Howth
Margaret Vandercook
Margaret W. Hungerford
Margret Penrose
Maria Edgeworth
Maria Thompson Daviess
Mariano Azuela
Marion Polk Angellotti
Mark Overton
Mark Twain
Mary Austin
Mary Catherine Crowley
Mary Cole
Mary Hastings Bradley
Mary Roberts Rinehart
Mary Rowlandson
M. Wollstonecraft Shelley
Maud Lindsay
Max Beerbohm
Myra Kelly
Nathaniel Hawthrone
Nicolo Machiavelli
O. F. Walton
Oscar Wilde

Owen Johnson
P.G. Wodehouse
Paul and Mabel Thorne
Paul G. Tomlinson
Paul Severing
Percy Brebner
Percy Keese Fitzhugh
Peter B. Kyne
Plato
Quincy Allen
R. Derby Holmes
R. L. Stevenson
R. S. Ball
Rabindranath Tagore
Rahul Alvares
Ralph Bonehill
Ralph Henry Barbour
Ralph Victor
Ralph Waldo Emmerson
Rene Descartes
Ray Cummings
Rex Beach
Rex E. Beach
Richard Harding Davis
Richard Jefferies
Richard Le Gallienne
Robert Barr
Robert Frost
Robert Gordon Anderson
Robert L. Drake
Robert Lansing
Robert Lynd
Robert Michael Ballantyne
Robert W. Chambers
Rosa Nouchette Carey
Rudyard Kipling
Saint Augustine
Samuel B. Allison
Samuel Hopkins Adams
Sarah Bernhardt
Sarah C. Hallowell
Selma Lagerlof
Sherwood Anderson
Sigmund Freud
Standish O'Grady
Stanley Weyman
Stella Benson
Stella M. Francis

Stephen Crane
Stewart Edward White
Stijn Streuvels
Swami Abhedananda
Swami Parmananda
T. S. Ackland
T. S. Arthur
The Princess Der Ling
Thomas A. Janvier
Thomas A Kempis
Thomas Anderton
Thomas Bailey Aldrich
Thomas Bulfinch
Thomas De Quincey
Thomas Dixon
Thomas H. Huxley
Thomas Hardy
Thomas More
Thornton W. Burgess
U. S. Grant
Upton Sinclair
Valentine Williams
Various Authors
Vaughan Kester
Victor Appleton
Victor G. Durham
Victoria Cross
Virginia Woolf
Wadsworth Camp
Walter Camp
Walter Scott
Washington Irving
Wilbur Lawton
Wilkie Collins
Willa Cather
Willard F. Baker
William Dean Howells
William le Queux
W. Makepeace Thackeray
William W. Walter
William Shakespeare
Winston Churchill
Yei Theodora Ozaki
Yogi Ramacharaka
Young E. Allison
Zane Grey

www.ingramcontent.com/pod-product-compliance
Lightning Source LLC
Chambersburg PA
CBHW030330180626
46810CB00003B/1295